Leadership Education and Training in China

Feng Jun   Zhen Jinzhou   Zhou Zhiping   Dai Zhenyu

Published by
ACA Publishing Ltd.
University House
11-13 Lower Grosvenor Place,
London SW1W 0EX, UK
Tel: +44 (0)20 7834 7676 Fax: +44 (0)20 7973 0076
E-mail: info@alaincharlesasia.com

Web: www.alaincharlesasia.com
Beijing Office
Tel:+86(0)10 8472 1250 Fax:86(0)10 5885 0639
Written by Feng Jun, Zhen Jinzhou, Zhou Zhiping, Dai Zhenyu
Edited by Sara Carvell, Martin Savery, ACA Publishing Ltd
Translated by Cai Junmei
© People's Publishing House, 2015
This translation is published by ACA Publishing Ltd in association with People's Publishing House

ALL RIGHTS RESERVED. NO PART OF THIS
PUBLICATION MAY BE REPRODUCED IN MATERIAL FORM,
BY ANY MEANS, WHETHER GRAPHIC,
ELECTRONIC, MECHANICAL OR OTHER, INCLUDING
PHOTOCOPYING OR INFORMATION STORAGE, IN
WHOLE OR IN PART, AND MAY NOT BE USED TO PREPARE
OTHER PUBLICATIONS WITHOUT WRITTEN
PERMISSION FROM THE PUBLISHER.

The greatest care has been taken to ensure accuracy but the publisher can accept no responsibility for errors or omissions, or for any liability occasioned by relying on its content.
ISBN 978-1-910760-05-5
Lerdaership Education and Training in China is available from the National Bibliographic Service of the British Library.

Preface

What is the state system of China? How has the Communist Party of China (CPC) managed to exercize long-term governance and to lead the Chinese people from one victory to another? What are the 'secrets' of the CPC's governance? What is China's development road? What significant strategies have been adopted in China? What is the next step in China's development? Why has China been able to achieve such rapid economic development? These are just some of the many questions frequently asked by the international community, especially foreign political parties and statesmen on their visits to China. For the purpose of providing answers to these questions and enabling readers to be informed about the real China and the CPC, we arranged for the *Understanding Modern China* Series (hereinafter referred to as the Series) to be written, to serve as elementary documents introducing the CPC, as well as China's development road, development theories and development experience.

The Series is inspired by the new philosophies, new ideas and new strategies for the country's governance put forward by General Secretary Xi Jinping since the 18th National Congress of the CPC, aimed at the following aspects: strenuously reflecting the development vision of 'the Chinese Dream' and the development prospects of the 'Two Centenary' goals; strenuously reflecting the coordinated promotion of the overall situation of a 'five-pronged approach to building socialism with Chinese characteristics to build up socialist economy, socialist democracy, socialist advanced culture, socialist harmonious society and socialist ecological civilisation; and the strategic arrangements for the 'Four-Pronged Comprehensive Strategy' comprehensively completing the building of a moderately prosperous society in all respects, comprehensively deepening reform in all respects, comprehensively advancing the rule of law, and comprehensively exercising strict discipline for the party; strenuously reflecting the 'new normal' facilitating and leading China's economic development and the implementation of the 'five major development concepts' to promote innovative, coordinated, green, open and shared development; strenuously reflecting the three major economic development strategies of the 'Belt and Road', the coordinated development of Beijing, Tianjin and Hebei province, and the Yangtze river economic belt. On the basis of a great number of fresh cases and experiences, the Series tells China's story, transmits China's voice, analyzes China's problems, and offers China solutions.

The Series has been written on the basis of telling China's story and transmitting China's voice, oriented around the following four aspects: the first is to illustrate the new measures taken to deepen reform since the 18th National Congress of the CPC, the new ideas on economic development and the new philosophy on foreign affairs, on the basis of an all-round introduction to the achievements since the reform and opening up; the second is to analyze the reason for the achievements, the underlying operating law, and the process of evolution, while presenting the development achievements of China's economy and society; the third is to keep to problem orientation and demand orientation, rather than attempt to be all-embracing and systematic, so as to clear up targeted doubts and confusion on the basis of the demands of foreign readers; the fourth is to introduce China not only in terms of 'where it is coming from', but also in terms of 'where it is going', for the purpose of enabling readers to know about China's historical development process on the one hand, and on the other hand, exemplifying and clarifying how China assures the organic unification of its past, present and future, the organic combination of legacy and innovation, and how China is planning its future development.

Under the guidance of the International Department of the CPC Central Committee, the writing of the Series has been organized by China Executive Leadership Academy Pudong (CELAP).

The International Department of the CPC Central Committee is the functional department of the CPC in charge of foreign affairs. So far, the CPC has established connections of various types with more than 600 political parties and organizations in over 160 countries and regions, which include left-wing and right-wing parties; both ruling parties and opposition parties. Foreign affairs work is of paramount importance to the CPC, and an indispensable component of national diplomacy as a whole, whose target is to promote state-to-state and people-to-people communication and understanding.

Preface

CELAP is a national leadership institution in China, and as a platform on which international cooperative training and exchange are carried out, CELAP has held fast to its characteristics of internationality and openness since March 2005 when it was founded. CELAP spares no effort in implementing international cooperative training, with target participants being foreign political parties and statesmen, high-ranking business executives and senior professionals. By the end of 2015, CELAP had offered training programs to more than 6,000 participants from over 130 countries, and thus has won wide recognition and received a favorable reception from the countries, regions and participants that are involved.

To cater for the needs of foreign participants, CELAP initiated the writing of the Series at the beginning of 2012, and after four years of modifications and improvements, the finalized manuscripts were completed at the end of 2015. The first batch of 10 books to be published in this Series are: *China's New Strategies for Governing the Country; The Communist Party of China: the Past, Present and Future of Party Building; China's Reform, Opening Up and Construction of Development Zones; The Framework of the Chinese Government and Public Services; A New Analysis of Urbanization in China; China's Agriculture and Rural Development in the Post-Reform Era; The Evolution of China's Diplomacy in the Modern Era; Leadership Selection and Appointment in China; Leadership Education and Training in China;* and *Shanghai – the 'Pacesetter' of China's Reform and Opening Up.*

The authors of the Series are mainly professionals in CELAP, and functionaries and specialists in the Development Research Center of the Shanghai Municipal People's Government, Shanghai Institute for International Studies and Hangzhou Research Center for Urban Studies.

The Series is published in Chinese and English, with the English translation done mainly by senior professors at Shanghai International Studies University, to whom thanks are due. Gratitude also goes to the People's Publishing House for its great support and positive suggestions in the process of writing and translating.

Writing such a series of textbooks for mature foreign students is a first in China. Constructive criticism is welcome, for the Series as a new endeavor can hardly be free from mistakes.

Editorial Committee of the *Understanding Modern China* Series
January 2016

The Editorial Committee of the Understanding Modern China Series

Directors: Guo Yezhou Feng Jun

Vice Directors: Zhou Zhongfei   An Yuejun

Members: (Listed alphabetically)

An Yuejun	Chen Zhong	Feng Jun
Guo Yezhou	He Lisheng	Jiang Haishan
Li Man	Li Yanhui	Liu Genfa
Liu Jingbei	Wang Guoping	Wang Jinding
Yang Jiemian	Zhao Shiming	Zheng Jinzhou
Zhou Zhenhua	Zhou Zhongfei	

Editor-in-Chief: Feng Jun

Alain Charles Asia (ACA) Publishing Ltd is delighted to be associated with the People's Publishing House to bring this series of 10 *Understanding Modern China* books to an English-speaking readership.

ACA, formerly known as ACP (Alain Charles Publishing) Ltd Beijing, was founded in October 1989 and was the first foreign-owned publishing company to be allowed to open an office in China.

In 2007, ACP Beijing was renamed ACA Publishing Ltd to better reflect its focus on China and the Asia-Pacific region. The company specialises in publishing books about China for international readers and has offices in Beijing and London.

ACA Publishing Ltd,

April 2016

Contents

Introduction IX
    I. Teaching Objectives IX
    II. Framework of the Book XII
    III. Reading Guidance XIII

1. Who Manages 1
    I. Management System 1
    II. Working Procedure 10
    III. Funds Management 12
    IV. Trainee Management 14

2. What to Learn 20
    I. Teaching Content 20
    II. Updating Content 25

3. How to Learn 34
    I. Educational Modules 34
    II. Teaching Methods 46

4. Where to Learn 55
    I. System of Training Institutions 56
    II. Training Base Construction 67
    III. Construction of Educational Discipline 75

5. Who Teaches 79
    I. Full-time Teaching Faculties 80
    II. Part-time Teachers 87

Conclusion 95

Chapter Follow-up Questions and References 101

Introduction

I. Teaching Objectives

Before going into the details of education and training, let us first take a look at the general conditions of contemporary China and the historical development of official (cadre)[1] education and training in the country.

China is an ancient civilization with a long history and splendid culture, with a land area of 9.6 million square kilometers, ranking third in the world. With over 1.3 billion people China is the most populous country. China is one of the five permanent members of the United Nations Security Council, together with the United States, Russia, the United Kingdom and France. China is also the world's second largest economy, with the largest foreign exchange reserves, as well as one of the fastest growing economies. All these great achievements have been made by the governance of the Communist Party of China (CPC) since 1949, particularly after the implementation of the reform and opening-up policy. It took the CPC only 30 years to lift 400 million Chinese people out of poverty, to feed 1.3 billion people with great success and in turn build a moderately prosperous society.

One naturally wonders how the CPC enhances its governing capacity and leads the Chinese people to make these achievements? One important factor is that the CPC has a high regard for, and is indeed exceptional at, learning and training. Since its creation in 1921, the CPC has made cadre education and training a fundamental and strategic way to improve its quality as a pioneer and competence as a governing party.

---

[1] The terms 'official' and 'cadre' are used interchangeably in this book, both referring to specially trained people in a profession, political party, or military force. Nonetheless, 'cadre' is more often used in reference to party leaders before the founding of the PRC, while 'official' covers a wider range of personnel after the founding of the PRC.

One of the most prominent features of China's cadre education is that all practices are supposed to serve the CPC's guidelines and central tasks with a focus on cultivating cadres' adaptability to the needs of revolutionary and state building campaigns. Throughout the 93-year history of the CPC, we divide China's cadre education and training into three stages, each ranging for about three decades.

The first stage is from the establishment of the CPC to the founding of the People's Republic of China (PRC) (1921-1949). Cadre education then was mainly for a revolutionary party that wisely realized since its inception that the training of cadres was a guarantee of success in its revolutionary pursuit. Despite difficult conditions, the CPC opened various institutions to teach and disseminate Marxism among party members and cadres in places like Hunan Self-Study University, Anyuan Party School, peasant movement learning centers, Shanghai University and other training institutions. During that time, cadre education primarily took the forms of full-time and on-the-job training. Although there were cadre training schools of different kinds, including the Central Party School, and the Anti-Japanese Military and Political College, and public schools in northern Shaanxi, it was impossible for most cadres to be full-time students due to poor conditions, pressing military combat and harsh circumstances in wartime. Cadres could only make use of limited time at intervals between battles to receive the necessary training while still on active service. It is undeniable that on-the-job training played a major role in preparing a large group of military and political talents for revolutionary campaigns and later political power building.

The second stage is between the period after the founding of the PRC and before the start of reform and opening up (1949-1978) when the CPC transformed from a revolutionary party into a governing party. Along with China's nation building, cadre (official) training also witnessed significant development. A network of party schools covering both the central and regional level emerged with a large group of cadres enrolled in party schools, universities and various technical schools, making a solid foundation for the socialist endeavor. However, party school education at that time was not adequately regulated and systematized.

The third stage is from the implementation of the reform and opening-up policy to the present (1978-2014). This new era of China's official education features standardization, legalization and a more scientific approach. First, a clear target and strategy are put forward. The CPC put official education and training in a more prominent position, making significant endeavors to build a Marxist governing party that is learning-oriented, service-oriented and innovation-oriented. The strategic task is to train officials on a large scale and enhance their quality in a tremendous way. Emphasis is put on strengthening their ideals and beliefs, enhancing their governing awareness and capacity. All efforts should be made to cultivate quality officials as those who are firm in belief, willing to serve the people, diligent, pragmatic, accountable, pure and honest. Second, China's official education and training have become more multi-leveled, multi-channeled and larger in scale. Significant improvements can be found in teaching facilities and teaching methods. A comprehensively constructed complex of official education and training institutions has been set up with emphasis on the establishment of party schools, schools of administration and leadership academies. At the national level, there are the Central Party School and the National School of Administration in Beijing. In 2005, three high-profile leadership academies were opened, located in Shanghai's Pudong District, Jinggangshan and Yan'an, respectively known as CELAP, CELAJ and CELAY.[2] There are party schools and schools of administration in each province, and party schools in each city or even county. According to statistics, there are over 4,500 official education and training institutions in China above the county level, including 3,100 party schools, 300 schools of administration, 400 cadre schools and 600 professional training centers under various departments. In all, 108,000 personnel have been involved in official education with participants (students/trainees) recently totaling 15 million each year, a scale second to none in the world. Third, official training and education has become increasingly regulated by law. A series of regulations have been promulgated including *Civil Servant Law of the PRC, Regulations on Official Education and Training Work, Regulations on CPC Party Schools* and *Reform Program for Official Education and Training from 2010 to 2020*. A working mechanism has been set up to chart out a Five-Year Plan on official education and training on the national level periodically in order to strengthen its guidance. A hierarchical management system has been established in the form of leading committees in different localities and a joint conference system, with the CPC Central Committee as the head, organizing departments as supervisors, and relevant divisions as implementers.

---

[2] China Executive Leadership Academy Pudong (CELAP)
China Executive Leadership Academy Jinggangshan (CELAJ)
China Executive Leadership Academy Yan'an (CELAY)

Western scholars have also been greatly attracted to conducting research on China's official education and training. Dr. Frank Pieke, an expert on contemporary China politics and social issues, who is also a University Lecturer of Modern Politics and Society of China and Fellow of St Cross College, University of Oxford, proposes in his book, *The Good Communist: Elite Training and State Building in Today's China*, that cadre training in China proves to be a powerful way to enforce management and control of government officials, and accordingly to promote modern administrative management. It is through this education and training that cadre students are required to emerge as more modern and capable officials with the ability to handle complex situations and tackle complicated conflicts.

The teaching objectives of this book are first to provide foreign students, through both systemic study and detailed description, with some knowledge on China's official education regarding management, training methods, institutional framework and some basic experience, and then to help them acquire insights into the CPC's practices. To put it simply, the purpose of this book is to address the five basic issues regarding Chinese official education and training, namely, Who to manage, What to learn, How to learn, Where to learn and Who teaches.

II. Framework of the Book

This book consists of five chapters.

Chapter 1 mainly introduces the management system of official education in China, including the systematic construction of training and administration institutions, scope of responsibility, and distribution and delimitation of power. Also stated in detail in this chapter are working procedure and budget management.

Chapter 2 elaborates on the contents of official education and training in China as to specific training programs, and the incorporation of major national development requirements into official training practice. Accordingly, the training contents have been constantly updated by keeping pace with the times.

Chapter 3 deals with effective training methods and various skills. It illustrates how China has learnt from and drawn on successful experiences at home and abroad to better its education of officials and to make it more pertinent and effective.

Chapter 4 is about training institutions for official education. Training bases are fundamental for promoting official education. Currently, they take shape in party schools, schools of administration and leadership academies. This chapter explains systematically their specific functions and particular advantages in official training.

Chapter 5 concerns the cultivation and management of the teachers of official training. To improve the quality of training, it is of key importance to develop teaching staff and faculties and maintain an adequate amount, comprehensive expertise and high quality. China has accumulated rich experience in faculty cultivation, team building and teacher selection, which are described in detail in this section.

III. Reading Guidance

Readers of this book are supposed to be foreign students who come to China to learn from our practice. Here are some suggestions for your comprehension and application of the information in this book.

First, read as much as you can to increase your understanding and appreciation of all aspects of China's circumstances. Make best use of the opportunity to study in China, to learn more about the country, its current development and the problems it has encountered. Only by doing so can you understand why China highly values official education and why we also require cadres and officials to study the contents just mentioned above.

Second, selectively draw on some of the essential practices and experiences from the book. Every nation has its own situation and development, and our official education is pertinent to our circumstances. We have combed through and summarized our practices, with the hope that they can be inspiring and helpful for you to turn them into applicable policies and measures in your country based on your national realities.

Last, please take the book *Chinapedia - The First Authoritative Reference to Understanding China* as your reference if you fail to understand some expressions or words with Chinese characteristics. In fact, while working on the book, we purposefully give a detailed introduction and explanation of some terms when they occur for the first time, and also endeavor to make some expressions comprehensible to you in your reading and understanding.

Chapter 1

Who Manages

I. Management System

As we all know, China is a large country with a vast territory and a huge population of over 1.3 billion. To run such a grand nation, a powerful governing team is of great necessity. It has been more than 60 years since the CPC took control of the government and started its mission as a ruling party. Ever since, the CPC has been attaching great importance to official education and training so as to provide batch after batch of key leaders and excellent talent for the causes of revolution, construction and reform in China. It is through the process of constant official education and training that the governing party is able to carry on its undertakings, with substantial support in terms of a robust ideological and political mentality and of competent leaders and intellectuals. It is a good tradition for the CPC to value learning and be good at learning, and this tradition plays a significant role in leading the Chinese government to successive accomplishments and secures the CPC's position as a governing party.

In January 2006, the CPC Central Committee issued *Regulations on Official Education and Training Work (Trial)* as party rules and as guidance for the work of official education and training. The *Regulations* stipulates that the training covers all officials of various levels and types, including party cadres, government officials, executives and administrators in enterprises, professionals and technicians, young or middle-aged officials, and grassroots officials. Furthermore, it requires that special attention be attached to training reserve cadres and officials above the county or division level owing to their positions and corresponding functions. In the operation of the political system of China, officials above the county or division level play an important role in undertaking causes of the party and the government, and they are outstanding talents in the society and capable leaders in various walks of life. Cadres' reserve is a source and an important supplement of the official team. To strengthen the construction of the current official team and its reserves is of strategic significance to ensure that the CPC will govern China for a long time and can do it well. What follows is a general introduction as to how the CPC conducts official education and training.

The management system of official education and training runs as a systematic arrangement of setting up administrative organs, assigning scopes of responsibility, and distributing and delimiting power under the leadership of the party and the nation.

Early in the Yan'an Period (the 13 years from 1935 to 1948 when the CPC Central Committee settled in northern Shaanxi), the CPC put forward the guidance explicitly that the work of official education and training should be conducted under the leadership of the CPC Central Committee and be administered by party committees and political bureaus of all levels, and by the Publicity and Education Department, hence resulting in some effective management systems. Since 1978 when the reform and opening-up policy commenced, the scope of training has been expanding, the scale of training has been enlarging, and the training burden has been growing heavier along with the continuous development of the party cause, which brings forth new requirements on official education and training for unified leadership and macro-management. Through a long struggle and practice, a hierarchical management system from the central to local administrations of official education and training with Chinese characteristics has come into being, in which the CPC Central Committee lies at the core, the party committees at all levels initiate general arrangements, and corresponding sectors take charge of specific works. The *Regulations on Official Education and Training Work (Trial)* states clearly that the national official education and training should be operated under the leadership of the CPC Central Committee, administered by the Organization Department, supervised by relevant divisions in the CPC Central Committee or the government, and managed hierarchically by its corresponding institutions.

1. The work of official education and training must be conducted under the leadership of the CPC Central Committee. The CPC is the only legal governing party in China. The party's leadership is exhibited in areas such as politics, the economy, society, culture, the military and diplomacy. Every undertaking of the party and the country must be implemented under the

guidance of the CPC Central Committee. Official education and training is an essential component of party building and the construction of a contingent of good officials. Once more, it must be reiterated that the undertaking of official education and training must be conducted under the leadership of the CPC Central Committee, by always keeping in line with the principle of cadres being managed by the party and official education and training also being administered by the party.

2. The Organization Department of the CPC Central Committee is in charge of organizational work, official management, and official education and training at the national level. Specifically, its functions are 'overall arrangement, macro-guidance, service coordination, supervision and inspection, and system regulation'.

Overall arrangement refers to a unified general arrangement and deployment of guidance, objectives and measures on official education and training, and official appointments within a certain period of time. To illustrate in detail, it includes such work as follows: in line with the guidelines, principles and policies of the CPC Central Committee, the Organization Department is responsible for drafting policies and opinions on national official education and training, arranging and deploying training plans, looking into the practice of official training activities and then putting forth relevant suggestions, and giving opinions on policies regarding teaching faculty, textbooks and funding. In order to promote official education and training, the Organization Department of the CPC Central Committee laid down and released a series of regulations successively in 1991, 1996, 2001, 2006 and 2013, and has formulated system standards with specific tasks and requirements as well as major feasible measures that are all scheduled at five-year intervals - well ahead of their implementation. The regulations concerned are *Key Points in the Plan for National Official Education and Training from 1991 to 1995, Plan for National Official Education and Training from 1996 to 2000, Plan for National Official Education and Training from 2006 to 2010,* and *Plan for National Official Education and Training from 2013 to 2017.*

Macro-guidance concerns proposing guiding opinions about how to implement principles and policies of the CPC Central Committee on official education and training conducted by departments and localities of all levels so as to promote this undertaking in those areas. The first is guidance for policies and theories. Based on conveying the spirit of some meetings of the CPC Central Committee as well as local realities, endeavors should be made to strengthen theoretical exploration in official education and training, launch corresponding policies, and propose explicit requirements on major tasks and important work related to this undertaking. The second is guidance for stratification and classification. In view of regional discrepancies in social development, guidance for official training should be applied differently to different areas such as the eastern, the middle or the western regions. According to the distinctive features of officials at different levels of province and ministry, city and bureau, county and division, and cadres in the general sense, we should put forward suitable suggestions and measures on the work of official education and training. We should also initiate guiding principles to strengthen official education, pertinent to different attributes of party cadres, government officials, executives in enterprises, professionals and officials in other fields. The third is guidance for demonstration and promotion. We should closely examine the grassroots work, sincerely study new situations, solve new problems emerging in their official education and training work, and find and summarize good experiences and practices so as to promote this undertaking from a small local scale to a national scale.

Service coordination is an important work of the management department in charge of official education and training which coordinates with the CPC Central Committee, national government departments and relevant sectors in cities and provinces to help implement training tasks in corresponding areas. It refers to both coordination and service. As to coordination, there are three tasks. One is to coordinate work between national and local levels to handle important training commissions together. For example, the joint conference among administrators of all levels is held every year to serve the purpose of studying and accommodating official education and training in different localities and of different levels so as to forge a unified force to carry on this undertaking. Another is to organize and pull together various forces to cope with significant work. For instance, to speed up the construction of three national leadership academies (CELAP, CELAJ and CELAY), a board of administrators for each academy has been set up to study and resolve big problems in the process. This work is headed by the Organization Department of the CPC Central Committee, with the participation of relevant national government departments, and together with the endeavors of Shanghai municipality, the provinces of Jiangxi and Shaanxi, and their influential enterprises. The final task is to coordinate comprehensive work, to dispose of problems or to settle conflicts usually occurring in official education and training. For example, the Organization Department sets up and carries out a thorough annual training and coordinating plan in order to ensure that officials from different localities do not repeat similar training either by the same training institution or by different ones. As to service, the management department should increase their service awareness, improve management methods, instantly obtain information about difficulties or problems in its subordinate departments in different areas, and then offer timely help and support to places, departments and training institutions in need. Various assistance and favorable policies regarding training projects, funds, teachers and textbooks are usually deployed to the central and western regions or other underdeveloped areas. The service also concerns giving full play to policy making and organizing advantages so as to provide a consultation service to training institutions in different localities or under the supervision of different departments.

Supervision and inspection are effective measures to enforce implementation and promotion of official education and training. They cover the following aspects: how the party principles are carried through in official education and training; how training plans are applied and realized; how the responsibility system is implemented; how relevant regulations are conformed to and brought into force. Supervision and inspection are carried out by a combination of complementary measures like random superior inspection and voluntary self-check, regular reports to superiors and peer reports on a specific subject, and investigation and notification.

Developing and perfecting system regulation is a long-term endeavor to guarantee and promote the work of official education and training. Through a long period of exploration, China has constituted a relatively comprehensive system of official education and training with the outcome of a series of regulations. Among them, the major ones are *Civil Servant Law of the PRC, Regulations on Official Education and Training Work (Trial), Regulations on CPC Party Schools, Regulations on Schools of Administration, Administrative Measures on CELAP, CELAJ and CELAY*; and the minor ones are *Reform Program for Official Education and Training from 2010 to 2020, Plan for National Official Education and Training from 2013 to 2017, Joint Conference on Official Education and Training*, and other opinions and regulations regarding full-time training, executive training, grassroots training, university training bases and overseas official training. These two sets of regulations complement and facilitate each other with a close link. The launch and implementation of these regulations steadily supports a speedy and healthy development of official education and training.

3. According to the functional division of their work, the CPC Central Committee and the state organs concerned are responsible for their corresponding official education and training work and guide the professional training of their respective system.

In accordance with the *Plan for National Official Education and Training from 2001 to 2005*, the CPC Central Committee and national departments concerned shoulder their specific responsibilities based on their practical work. Responsible for officials' theoretical study, the Publicity Department of the CPC Central Committee organizes training for the backbone of the leadership in publicity and culture systems. The Ministry of Personnel guides and coordinates civil servants' training and the further education of professionals, and works out relevant policies and regulations. The National Development and Reform Commission (NDRC) checks and approves major projects concerning the national-level official education and training bases. The Ministry of Finance formulates official education and training funding policies, and provides financial support. The Work Committee for Offices Directly under the CPC Central Committee, and State Organs Work Committee of the CPC, based on their respective functions, are in charge of relevant official education and training work. Other departments of the CPC Central Committee and state organs take charge of official education and training in their respective departments. They all provide operational guidance for official education and training and direct the work centering on professional knowledge.

4. Local party committees of all levels guide their corresponding local official education and training work. They implement the official education and training policies and guidelines of the party and the state, bring official education and training into line with the local economic and social development plan, and study and arrange local training work. The organization departments of local party committees of all levels are in charge of local official education and training. The departments concerned of the local party committees and governments at all levels are responsible for their corresponding work in official education.

Local party committees of all levels have the following duties. First, they carry out the party's policies and guidelines on official education and training, implement the major deployments proposed by the CPC Central Committee, and fulfill all official training and education tasks by continuously following the correct official education and training direction. Second, they bring official education and training into line with the local social development plan. When formulating the economic and social development program, local party committees of all levels should consider the importance of official education and training, and put forward work objectives, principles, tasks and measures on the basis of the local economic and social demands. When determining major projects on economic and social development and funding arrangements, they should give overall consideration, take various supporting measures, strengthen the construction of official education and training institutions and teaching staff, and guarantee the training funds investment in order to create favorable conditions for official education and training. Third, they should study and arrange local official education and training. Local party committees of all levels should study local official education and training work at regular intervals. The party and government principal leaders should listen to reports on official education and training, solve existing problems and make great efforts to accomplish each task. As required by the CPC Central Committee, they should combine local reality with the carrying out of tasks creatively to improve pertinence and effectiveness in implementing the CPC Central Committee's relevant policies and guidelines.

The organization departments of local party committees of all levels are in charge of local official education and training. Their specific duties can refer to the relevant duties of the Organization Department of the CPC Central Committee. The relevant departments of the local party committees and governments at all levels can refer to the division of duties regarding official education and training of the departments concerned. Under the leadership of the local party committee, the organization department of the same level should cooperate with the party committee to conduct relevant official education and training work.

5. The unit where officials work, according to official management authority, is responsible for this unit's official education and training. The *Regulations on Official Education and Training Work (Trial)* explicitly stipulates the unit's duties for official education and training. The unit plays a dominant role in official education and training, functioning as the organizer, implementer and promoter of various types of training at all times. Among officials of all ranks, only a small part (mainly leading officials at different levels) can participate in full-time training in such institutions as party schools, leadership academies and schools of administration. A majority of officials take their education and training as organized and

implemented by their work units. Currently, a growing trend in the practice of official education and training is to bring education into line with the unit's development plan and constantly strengthen autonomous training. The units attach increasing importance to official education and training. A unit has the following duties. First, it carries out the party's policies and guidelines in official education and training, and arranges and implements its own official education and training work by integrating with local reality. Second, it implements the work deployment of the party committee of a higher level and the official full-time training plan formulated by official education and training management departments of higher levels, and fulfills its own refresher training tasks. Third, based on its own work demands and officials' training needs, it selects and appoints officials by stages and in groups to participate in various types of full-time training. Fourth, it makes general requirements on officials' on-the-job self-study, helps them work out their learning plan and evaluates their performance. Fifth, it establishes and implements its own incentive and restriction mechanism of official education and training to ensure the implementation of each training task. Sixth, it increases financial investment in official education and training and creates favorable training conditions for its own officials.

6. The official education and training work managed by both department and locality can be organized by either side as a main force and assisted by the other based on their agreement. The former performs major functions in official management, and the latter assists the work as a subsidiary force. In November 1991, the Organization Department of the CPC Central Committee issued the *Circular on Several Issues Concerning the Dual Management of Officials* which prescribes both the duty and authority of the two forces in official dual management. The *Circular* stipulates that in dual management, if the departments of the CPC Central Committee play a principal role, one of the duties of their leading party groups (party committees) is to take charge of officials' political and theoretical study and training, officials' post training and various professional training sessions, and then local party committees simply give assistance. If the dual management in official management is implemented with the local committee playing the principal role, its duty is to take charge of officials' political and theoretical training. The CPC Central Committee assists them to guide and plan officials' post training and various professional training sessions in their own systems and to arrange the implementation of training tasks. In light of the principle of 'the one who takes charge conducts training', the major party who plays a

principal role is responsible for managing the training work, laying down the training plan and implementing training tasks. The assisting party offers help to a certain extent. Based on the two parties' consensus, the assisting party can take charge of part of the official education and training tasks entrusted by the major party. The assisting party brings the entrusted tasks into line with its local official training plan, makes overall plans and reasonable arrangements, and informs the other party of the current training conditions. The major party selects and appoints trainees, and creates favorable conditions for the assisting party to fulfill training tasks.

7. In official education and training, a joint conference system is implemented. In order to strengthen coordination and macro-guidance on official education and training, the CPC has established a joint conference system of official education. The *Plan for National Official Education and Training from 1996 to 2000* requires that we must 'establish a joint conference system of official education', and the proposal which supported this was passed on December 27, 1997, in the first meeting of the national education joint conference. In line with this system, a joint conference is held once or twice every year. The Official Education Bureau of the Organization Department of the CPC Central Committee is in charge of the joint conference's daily contact. The major tasks of the joint conference are to inform participants of the instructing spirit of the CPC Central Committee and State Council concerning official education, to study the implementation measures, to strengthen guidance and macro-guidance, to exchange information and discuss problems, and to promote this undertaking. There are 12 members in the joint conference. They are the Organization Department of the CPC Central Committee, the Publicity Department of the CPC Central Committee, the Party School of the CPC Central Committee, CELAP, CELAJ, CELAY, the NDRC, the Ministry of Human Resources and Social Security, the Ministry of Education, the Ministry of Finance, the State-owned Assets Supervision and Administration Commission (SASAC) of the State Council, and the Chinese Academy of Governance. As of 2013, 13 national official education joint conferences have been held, playing an important role in driving official education and training work. This management layout is suited to China's basic conditions and sticks to the basic principle that 'the party manages officials and the party manages official education', which helps form a united whole and implement the major policy decisions of the CPC Central Committee and party committees at all levels.

II. Working Procedure

After the introduction of the management system for education and training, we will make a detailed analysis on the working procedure of official education and training.

The entire operation process involves four relevant parties, namely, organization departments, officials' work units, training schools or institutions and official trainees themselves, with each shouldering their own responsibilities. For instance, organization departments are responsible for supervising, training institutions for running training programs on their own, work units for deciding on training participants, and official trainees for choosing and taking courses. The entire training process involves surveying needs, planning schedules, implementing programs, evaluating and giving feedback with each link closely connected to complete the loop. It is through rigorous exploration and reflection on laws governing the development and training of officials that we have now come to a relatively standard working procedure.

1. Identifying training needs through research and analysis. There are different types of analyses covering three levels of needs, respectively from an organization department, from a specific post and from officials themselves, conducted by their relevant parties with varying emphasis.

   Organization departments should look into organizational needs. The management department in charge of training and managing officials should analyze new requirements of officials' qualifications for handling new challenges in the newly developed party cause, collect information on the basic conditions of officials, identify prospective participants in need of training, and find out what training programs interest them and they want to participate in so as to develop suitable training programs and put them into practice.

   Work units that trainees are affiliated to are responsible for needs analyses on specific organizational demands from different posts, from different levels and from different types of officials. They are also responsible for an analysis of the gap between job requirements and officials' current command of knowledge and skills in order to decide who to train and what courses to take.

   Training institutions undertake the task of analyzing the needs of the organization department, work units and officials themselves in order to develop better training projects and courses.

Only with concerted efforts can the needs concerned be brought to light and put together to work out training plans which satisfy the demands of all relevant parties.

2. Working out training plans. This work concerns officials themselves and efforts of three parties, namely, management departments, training institutions and officials' work units. Specifically, their task allocations are as follows: the authority over official training is responsible for coordinating all relevant management departments to design training plans; work units that officials serve integrate work demands with officials' realities to work out their own training scheme; training institutions then decide on training programs catering to demands from officials and their work units. In addition, there are two approaches to plan creation, top-down and bottom-up. The former is task-oriented focusing on orders and tasks from the training authority, while the latter is client-oriented to produce training plans according to market demands. Close communication and cooperation among all three parties can enhance the efficiency and feasibility of training plans, reflecting the needs of all relevant parties.

3. Implementation. According to the settled training plan, the management department comes to finalize projects or classes, put forward requirements, organize participants, and select implementers through comparison or bidding in order to maximize training benefits. Accordingly, training institutions then make arrangements on specific programs, contents, curricula, teachers, teaching methods and other services. Management departments, training institutions, work units and official participants as trainees all play their respective role in fulfilling their tasks to accomplish training objectives through close communication and attendance supervision.

4. Evaluation. The management department and officials' work units usually do a holistic evaluation on trainees' performance, and take its results as an important basis for the selection or promotion of officials to activate their enthusiasm for training. The authority over official training is in charge of supervising evaluation, inspecting and guiding training to guarantee that evaluation results reflect teaching and learning realities, and to motivate training institutions to carry out their endeavors. So far, there have been some worthwhile experiences coming from nationwide practices. They are the regular inspection and appraisal of training schools, emphasis on the assessment of trainees' learning performance and achievements,

a systematic practice of reporting, commenting, and testing on training contents. Meanwhile, evaluation from official trainees and feedback through talks, as well as performance evaluation, all strengthen the assessment on teaching and training qualities, and provide reference and bases for improving teaching methodology, updating training contents and improving training quality and efficiency.

5. Providing feedback. An information data bank should be set up to keep a record on the training and assessment of official trainees, and to develop official training into an important channel of identifying, assessing, inspecting and cultivating potential leaders. The practice of associating training with officials' annual evaluation, rewards and awards, position promotion and welfare significantly incentivizes officials to participate in training. For instance, the Ministries of Finance and Agriculture have made participation in training a prerequisite for post competition.

III. Funds Management

Official education and training is a basic input with low cost and quick results. It is also a productive investment with big economic and social benefits. Strengthening official education and training is a vital component both in the strategy of rejuvenating China through science and education and in the strategy of reinvigorating China through human resource development. Requisite fund security is the premise and foundation on which official education and training runs smoothly, and it is an important condition to promote the constant development of official education and training.

1. Setting up a multi-channel fund input mechanism

First, it is necessary to include official education and training funds in the financial budget of governments at all levels. The nature of official education and training determines its funds, which mainly come from the financial budget of governments at all levels. The *Regulations on Official Education and Training Work (Trial)* stipulates that official education and training funds should be included in the annual financial budget of governments at all levels and used by the competent Department of Official Education and Training. The Organization Department proposes the budget and expenditure program according to the official education and training annual plan. The department of finance includes the funds in the annual budget and appropriates them on a timely basis.

Second, it is necessary to increase official education and training fund input step by step with fiscal revenue growth. The *Regulations on Official Education and Training Work (Trial)* stipulates that 'the proportion of educational appropriations in gross national product allocated by the state shall gradually rise, as the national economy develops and financial revenue increases'. As required, official education and training fund input should gradually rise as the financial revenue increases. However, the conditions vary in different localities and departments and the economic development levels differ greatly, so a uniform requirement on fund input is not put forward.

Third, it is necessary to broaden the channels of official education and training fund input. At present, China's official education and training funds mainly depend on financial revenues, which is a unitary input channel. In some underdeveloped areas, fund input is insufficient and unable to meet the needs of official education and training work. Based on its reality, each locality and each department can enact the appropriate standard on the premise that official education and training work can be carried out properly. It can establish the input system with the country, unit and individual included. The proportion of the three parties' fund input can be determined by the training time, cycle and methods of the party and government officials. The domestic non-governmental organizations (NGOs), units and individuals are encouraged to take various measures to provide funds for official education and training. If possible, funds from foreign governments, international institutions and transnational corporations for overseas official education and training programs can be accepted. Training institutions are supported to undertake training entrusted by society, enterprises and the market so as to broaden the source channels of official education and training funds.

2. Setting up a fund using a highly effective mechanism

The establishment of a reasonable training fund using a mechanism. The cost of planned classes, key training classes and important overseas training projects, and the cost of facilities construction in official education and training institutions should be provided by the department of finance. The expenditure of a single project should be provided by both the state and the unit. The degree and ability training which is not completely relevant to the post but relevant to an individual's career development can be funded by both the unit and the individual. An individual account operation mechanism for official education and training funds has been established. The official's individual account is set up. The annual official training funds are allocated to individual officials. On the basis of charging standards, the training is charged. The part of expenditure of various training sessions at different levels, which should be covered by officials, is appropriated from their individual accounts. A training voucher system can also be set up. Officials who participate in training this year can be given training vouchers. Training institutions gain training fees according to how many training vouchers they have received. Expenditure and training performance are linked to achieving the aim of promoting training institutions to improve training quality, and of achieving the efficient use of official training funds.

3. Establishing and perfecting an official education and training fund supervision mechanism

Setting a uniform charging standard. The official education and training department in charge, together with the price department, department of finance and official training colleges, formulates the uniform charging provisions on training fees and charging standards. Exclusive official education and training fund accounts are set up. Correspondingly, an audit system is in operation to closely monitor the expenditure of training funds so as to optimize their application.

IV. Trainee Management

To implement student (official trainee) management guarantees the fulfillment of teaching plans and attainment of teaching objectives. Party schools, leadership academies and cadre schools of all levels have obtained valuable experience and achieved favorable results.

1. Implementing orientation education. Once officials enter training schools, they are required to attend an orientation class to get to know teaching plans, objectives, requirements and teaching methods. In order to get them engaged in training wholeheartedly, schools should help official trainees to turn as soon as possible from leaders into learners, from a working mentality to a learning state, and from a family life to a collective school life.

2. Staying firm with discipline management. Official trainees should be treated fairly in accordance with various regulations and nine students' disciplines (see below) prescribed by the Organization Department of the CPC Central Committee. Those who misbehave or violate regulations should be punished resolutely without exception.

3. Strengthening training management. To achieve this purpose, a series of actions are taken as follows: cultivating a good learning atmosphere, activating learning incentives, strengthening teaching organization, keeping records of class attendance, arranging seminars, forums and activities for students' involvement, urging students to finish their study reports and the party spirit analysis, and guiding official trainees to take part in various recreational and sports activities.

4. Reinforcing party spirit education. Education in party spirit and discipline enforcement are carried through the whole training process. Upon entering a training institution, official trainees are required to make an individual and a collective study plan on exercising party spirit that will be assessed and graded later by self-checking and peer evaluation. The efforts taken attempt to make official trainees behave as communist party members with strict discipline and as common students observing school provisions.

5. Being strict with students' assessment. For each official trainee, a student record is set on their study and life in school. Before their graduation, a comprehensive assessment on their class attendance, learning process and practice of party spirit will be carried out, and the results will go as training feedback to the trainee's work unit and the relevant superordinate organization.

Provisions of the Organization Department of the CPC Central Committee on Further Strengthening Student Management in Official Education and Training

1. No matter what level they are at, officials are common trainees when they participate in training. They should adopt the correct attitude towards learning, establish the awareness of being trainees, and strictly observe training rules. They should be pure, honest, self-disciplined, focused on learning and earnest in fulfilling training tasks. The official management departments and official education and training institutions should put forward specific requirements on training officials.

2. During the training period, officials should live in the dormitory and have meals in the canteen. Neither trainees nor teachers can entertain each other by using public funds. Classes and groups should not enjoy banquets together in the name of group activity. Trainees should not take part in any dinner, banquet or entertainment activities which might affect

the impartial execution of their duties. Those who violate regulations should be expelled from school.

3. When they go out for activities like on-the-spot teaching and field investigation, trainees should not ask police cars to lead the way. They should take a buffet or light meal instead of accepting invitations to dinners. They should not accept souvenirs or local specialties, and should not arrange any travel or entertainment activities irrelevant to learning. If certain trainees violate regulations, the leaders of their training institution and those in charge of the team will be punished.

4. Trainees are not allowed to accept or present gifts, cash, marketable securities, disbursement vouchers or local specialties. They should not accept any courtesy visit. Trainees should not invite one another to travel in the name of learning exchange, counterpart visit, cross investigation, or collective research. Those who violate the rules will be punished in accordance with the seriousness of the case in the following ways: warning interviews, circulation of a notice of criticism, and being expelled from school. Trainees who accept or present precious gifts, cash, marketable securities or disbursement vouchers will be reported to the official management departments and their units, and will be dealt with in accordance with the regulations.

5. During the training period, trainees should not undertake tasks in their unit, such as work, meetings and visits abroad. If they need to ask for leave for special reasons, they should strictly follow the leave procedures. If the accumulated leave time exceeds 1/7 of the total period, they will be treated as having dropped out. Those who leave school without permission will be expelled from school.

6. Trainees must write speeches, their experience of study, an investigation report and a thesis by themselves. They are not allowed to employ ghostwriters, to plagiarize or to be accompanied by secretaries. Those who violate the regulations will be punished in accordance with the seriousness of the case, such as cancelling scores, circulating a notice of criticism or being expelled from school.

7. During the training period, trainees should not keep government vehicles in school, or borrow and keep another unit's or individual's vehicle in school. Those who violate the regulations will be punished via circulation of a notice of criticism.

8. During or after training, trainees are not allowed to form 'little cliques' in the name of classmates, to set up any syndicate or fellow-students association, or to develop organized activities with fixed conveners and contacts. They are not allowed to take advantage of classmate relations to provide convenience for each other and obtain profits for themselves with respect to official appointments, personnel arrangements, and their children's education, employment or business dealings. Among those who violate the regulations during training, the initiator will be expelled from school, and the rest of the participants will be criticized by circulating a notice. Those who have completed the training will be investigated and dealt with by the relevant departments.

9. The management departments of official education and training along with training institutions should practice rigid economy and practice frugality in running the school. They are not allowed to hold training classes in high-class hotels and scenic and historic areas, to arrange luxurious accommodation, nor to distribute expensive giveaways and souvenirs. It is strictly prohibited to travel at public expense in the name of training. If the rules are violated, the leaders of the sponsoring organizations will be investigated and held accountable.

Case 1 CELAP's Experience in Managing Official Trainees

In terms of the management of its trainees, CELAP has formed a set of effective practices and mechanisms, featuring professional running of classes and operating procedures, precise management of human resources and information-assisted methods. For a thorough implementation of the *Regulations on Strengthening the Management of Trainees in Official Education and Training (The Regulations)* issued by the Organization Department of the CPC Central Committee, we have established a leading group for creating a good learning environment headed by the executive vice president, through studying work projects and a systematic implementation and promotion of trainee management and learning environment construction.

1. Discipline trainees with various measures. We strengthen education by publicizing the full text of *The Regulations* on all kinds of information platforms such as the trainee manual, the college electronic information platform and electronic screens, by putting *The Regulations* and the alert cards of *Trainees Discipline* in their dormitories, and by reinforcing the publicity and interpretation of these regulations in the orientation

course. In these ways, we have created a publicity environment for a good learning atmosphere. Class advisors or teachers in charge are required to learn the details of rules by heart, to constantly remind trainees, to administrate and supervise them strictly and to implement the regulations rigorously. We stress key factors and supervise their attendance strictly. The multifunctional card is used to strengthen supervision and obtain feedback on trainees' accommodation, entry and exit. Trainees are required to punch in when they take lessons, have meals, and enter and leave the college, which aims to ensure that all lessons are checked and all trainees are recorded. In order to improve the safeguard measures for trainees on campus and build a defensive line for safety, we use every effort to promote our ability to tackle emergencies by making contingency plans and finding out vulnerable and risky parts in the training process.

2. Sincerely and thoroughly conduct reflections on party spirit. According to the notification and requirement of the Organization Department of the CPC Central Committee, every class involving highlighted programs conducts the party spirit analysis around the theme of 'self-purification against four types of corrupting tendencies (formalism, bureaucratism, hedonism and extravagance)'. Accordingly, every trainee should write documents on party spirit, make personal statements and mutual comments in the party group, summarize their own conduct and communicate in the official trainees' party branch while integrating the latest strategy and decisions of the CPC Central Committee as well as training topics with their own personal growth. All of these practices have achieved good effects. Comrade Zhao Leji, President of CELAP, comments that "these practices are well done. Please summarize and continue". Every semester, we organize trainees to study the spirit of Minister Zhao Leji's speech delivered in the opening ceremony, to analyze and examine the problems not only in their ideology, beliefs, outlook on life, the world, and values, but also in their learning about Marxism and connecting theory with practice, and to enhance the pertinence and effects of the analytical activities of the party spirit.

3. Vigorously advocate the Marxist style of study, and uphold the spirit of integrating theory with practice. We put much emphasis on guiding trainees to get involved in the training with questions and take lessons while integrating reality, and guide them to research on special subjects around the teaching themes as well. We also organize classes to make achievements in research on special subjects and constantly promote the

effects of training. To run classes more professionally, we set up project groups around the training topic and appoint department leaders and section chiefs to preside over the training and research work on these topics so as to promote it. Before the training, we must make early contact with the Department of Teaching and Research and have early contact with trainees when sending out information for admission. The 'two brought-in' materials of the trainees are required to be closely connected with the major practical problems, the training topics and the training plans. In the training, we ask the teachers who are class cadres to lead trainees to learn with practice and ask all the classes to write research summaries and reports carefully. All the trainees must take part in the process, have in-depth communication, hold discussions actively and pool all of the beneficial thoughts together. After the training, we must attach importance to the summary and extraction of the results and effects in the management of classes. Integrating the reality of regions and departments, we find ideas to solve problems and promote pertinent policy and suggestions after our learning and researching the advanced theories and important ideas around the training topic in order to reduce and resolve temporary problems. We promote the research class of special subjects to make achievements in practical work and to produce quality reports on decision making and consultation by educating, training and researching collectively.

4. Create a positive and healthy campus cultural atmosphere. To enrich trainees' after-school life, we offer optional courses such as literature and arts expositions and fitness practice, set up 'Hujiang bookshelves' in the library and dormitory reading corners in cooperation with Hujiang online school in Shanghai, and organize reading activities extensively among trainees. In the 'Academic's Salon' trainees demonstrate their talent and appraisal of the arts while taking full advantage of the talent gathered together in the senior expert class to create opportunities for the enjoyment of beauty, and to forge a platform for the appreciation of fine art by integrating all kinds of sophisticated art resources into the academy. The activity for the appreciation of fine art is held every month to make campus life more interesting and to promote officials' artistic taste. This activity is highly recognized and widely welcomed by official trainees.

Chapter 2

What to Learn

Teaching contents and curricula are the key to official education activities, and are also important in realizing the goal of official education. In this chapter, we will analyze how official training contents are designed and updated to deepen your understanding of this topic.

I. Teaching Content

According to the *Regulations on Official Education and Training Work (Trial)*, official education and training should take into consideration the needs of economic and social development, the requirement of facilitating the improvement of the ruling capacity of the party and maintaining the advanced position of the party, as well as the demands of the post and characteristics of officials at different levels and of different categories. The basic contents of official education should include political theory, party spirit, policies and regulations, professional knowledge, cultural literacy, specific skills and global vision, with a particular focus on political theory.

1. Education on political theory. In order to improve the ideological and political quality of leaders and officials, the development of their Marxist theoretical capability is prioritized. Basic principles of Marxism include Marxism-Leninism and Mao Zedong Thought. We need to educate and guide officials to deepen their understanding of the essence of Marxism-Leninism and Mao Zedong Thought, to enable them to master their fundamental rules and their scientific system, and to deepen their understanding of the rules and governance of the party, building a socialist society and the social development of human beings. Efforts should also be made to help officials develop a firm belief in Marxism and a capacity to analyze and solve problems from a Marxist viewpoint

and methods. At the current stage, we need officials to thoroughly study the theoretical system of socialism with Chinese characteristics, including Deng Xiaoping Theory, the important thinking of the Three Represents, the Scientific Outlook on Development and the guiding principles from Comrade Xi Jinping's major speeches. Officials should be educated and guided to further understand the scientific connotations, spiritual essence and fundamental requirements of socialism with Chinese characteristics so as to strengthen their confidence in the path, theory and system of socialism with Chinese characteristics. Special efforts should be made to help officials develop a deeper understanding of the spiritual essence of the Scientific Outlook on Development and push further their initiatives and practice. The study of the theoretical system of socialism with Chinese characteristics should be combined with the study of classic Marxist works, along with that of the dynamic practices of reform and opening up, and the modernization drive.

2. Education on the party's history, spirit and discipline, as well as China's situation. In line with the requirement of strengthening the party's governing capacity and keeping its advanced position, as well as the realities of officials' mindset, efforts should be made specifically to promote the study of the party's constitution, history, tradition and discipline, with a focus on the Marxist view of the masses and education on the party's mass line, in order to consolidate officials' Marxist outlook on the world and power, as well as on their careers and their awareness of being public servants. On discipline education, emphasis should be placed on resolutely fighting against the corrupting tendencies of formalism, bureaucractism, hedonism and extravagance. In terms of anti-corruption education, officials should increase their ability to resist corruption and prevent misconduct. Education on the history of the party and the country, in particular of the crucial periods of revolution, development, reform and opening up, conducted by the people under the leadership of the CPC, enables officials to develop an understanding of the complete development of the origins of the party and the country, and remain conscientiously loyal to the party and the country.

3. Policy and regulation. This education should focus on the party's lines and policies as well as national laws and regulations, and carry out training on the major strategies and requirements of the party and the country in various areas such as the economy, politics, culture, society, diplomacy

and national defense to ensure that officials practice governance that is based on law scientifically and democratically. Policy and regulation education has always been an important part of official training and education, as policy and strategy are the lifeline of the party. The party and government officials are organizers and leaders who are required to accomplish the tasks of the party and the nation, and are responsible for the implementation of the party's line, principles, policies and plans, as well as the laws of the country. Policy and regulation education should cover three major aspects: the party's line, principles and policies, the important plans of the party and the nation, and national laws and regulations. First, the party's line, principles and policies reflect the essential theories of the party in different historical periods and under different circumstances. They are the generalization and summary of new practices, and act as a guide for conduct. This aims to help officials acquire the correct knowledge of the party's principles and policies, its spiritual essence, and the overall interest of the nation, and constantly improve their capability to implement the party's line, principles and policies. Second, the party and the nation work out important plans in every historical period to accommodate new conditions and tasks, which are then conveyed to officials through training facilities. Officials should develop a deep and concise understanding of these plans and implement them accordingly. Third, national laws and regulations, including the constitution, statutes, governing rules, local administrative provisions and professional regulations are the bases for running and governing the country by law. Training should help officials improve their capacity to make decisions, exercise their duties and manage affairs based on these national laws and regulations.

4. Professional knowledge. This education aims to help officials acquire the knowledge required to fulfill their duties competently as experts and leaders. First, the contents of the training should be combined with the professional knowledge required from the position, as each job has its specific requirements, professional knowledge and ability which varies from those of other posts. Efforts should be made to conduct training that is orientated to meeting the demands of the post, to help trainees integrate knowledge with practice and attune the growth of their capability to improvement of their work, but to keep away from training that is detached from reality and the actual needs of the post in order to enhance their capability and help

officials carry out their job responsibilities. Second, in line with rapid developments in science and technology, training should include new thoughts, theories, knowledge, and rules to help officials systematically update and improve their knowledge structure. Third, types of training should be categorized with different contents to suit the requirements of different professions and posts. These professions and posts are classified into three types according to their nature, attributes, and management requirements. These types are comprehensive management, special technology, and administration and law enforcement. Comprehensive management focuses on public management, leadership science and sociology. Special technology involves the knowledge and technique of a particular industry. Education on administration and law enforcement focuses on professional knowledge as well as laws and administrative regulations, in order to enhance officials' governing capacity based on law.

5. Training on cultural literacy. Efforts are made to improve officials' knowledge structure and to improve their comprehensive quality, with a focus on literacy in science and liberal arts. Regarding science, we supply training on scientific knowledge, spirit and methodology to strengthen officials' awareness of science and laws in science, cultivate a scientific way of thinking and improve their ability to innovate, in order to meet the requirements for building an innovation-oriented country that adapts to global developments in science and technology. As to liberal arts, the goal is to cultivate officials' sentiment towards liberal arts and enhance their taste in fine art through the study of literature, art, history and philosophy. In recent years, some training institutions and organization departments have arranged many cultural activities popular among officials, including lectures on history, culture, symphony, folk music and Peking Opera.

6. Skills training. The skills concerned refer to techniques as well as the capacity to apply scientific knowledge and practical experience in the workplace. This includes methods, experience, techniques, crafts and ways of thinking that can be acquired through training. Training in these techniques has been widely implemented with the purpose of cultivating civil servants in foreign countries such as Germany and Canada, covering topics on professional methods and techniques, settling disputes and conflicts, functioning as administrators, using public media, interaction and communication. For China, with the development of science and

technology, its policy of opening up to the outside world and the shift of government functions, requirements for various skills are becoming higher and higher for officials. Recently, relevant institutions conducted training in foreign languages, computers and the art of leadership, achieving satisfactory results. Skills training varies much in contents and covers a wide scope, but can be generalized into two categories based on their professional requirements: one is general skills, and the other is special skills for particular jobs. The first concerns document writing, the science of public management, and social conduct and etiquette, and should be mastered by officials in general. The second type of skills, which are targeted at officials of different types, at different levels and in different posts include the art of decision-making, skills regarding how to respond to the media, and skills to cope with public crises and emergencies. Skills training may help officials learn advanced and applicable techniques, improve their practical skills, and become more competent in their duties.

7. Education on global vision and intercultural communication. Given the backdrop of globalization and China opening up to the outside world, we should provide officials with training that is focused on new trends of world development, modern international relations, and important current issues, as well as on China's foreign policies, strategic moves, diplomatic policies, international law, charters and provisions of international organizations, and the successes or failures experienced by developed countries and newly-emerging countries. CELAP has made successful endeavors to broaden China's global vision and improve the intercultural communicative abilities of its official participants through several methods. First of all, world-renowned professors, experts and scholars are invited to teach them how to resolve China's domestic economic and social issues with overseas experience and lessons. In highlighted programs, this kind of practice takes up 10-15% of the curriculum. Second, in order to broaden participants' understanding of a particular issue, domestic experts are invited to conduct an international comparative study. Third, official participants are sent to study abroad. All efforts are made to help officials obtain knowledge on global situations and enhance their capability in handling international affairs and coordinating China's domestic and international actions.

II. Updating Content

The need to update official education and training content. The rich, updated and complete training content and innovative training curriculum are both the inevitable choice to promote the teaching reform of official education and training, to adapt to economic and social development, and to improve the pertinence and effectiveness of official education and training.

First, establishing the official education and training content updating mechanism is an objective requirement to thoroughly implement the Scientific Outlook on Development and achieve the goal of building a generally well-off society. In this new era, China has opened a new chapter in its development. The CPC has publicized the Scientific Outlook on Development, which is based on scientific analysis and the characteristics of China's current development. The Scientific Outlook on Development embodies Marx's doctrine about the developing world outlook and methodology, and serves as the important guiding ideology of China's economic and social development. At the 18th National Congress of the CPC, the Scientific Outlook on Development was added to the *Constitution of the CPC* as a long-term guiding ideology that the CPC must adhere to. In order to thoroughly implement the Scientific Outlook on Development in the party, it is an objective requirement to innovatively improve training content and update training courses in official education and training. Additionally, the latest theoretical achievements in the localization of Marxism in China must be systematically incorporated into textbooks, vividly conveyed in the classroom and, as a result, effectively learned by officials.

Second, establishing a content updating mechanism is an objective requirement to build a political party that is oriented toward the study of Marxism. This means the party should systematically learn scientific theory and advanced knowledge so as to enhance the vitality of the party. The foundation for building a study-oriented political party must be that the party's officials study effectively. Besides grasping the party's fundamental theories, party officials should widely study philosophy, history and China's traditional culture, increase their knowledge of the modern market economy, modern international relations, and modern management. They should also adopt new skills in order to improve their strategic, innovative and dialectic thinking ability, which they can then apply at work. Therefore, it is an objective requirement for us to constantly update both the training content and curriculum, ensuring that they are suitable for building a Marxist study-oriented political party.

Third, establishing a content updating mechanism is an objective requirement for adapting to the current state of China's economic and social development, serving the general aims of the party and the state, and for promoting the comprehensive, coordinated and sustainable development of the economy and society. The world today is undergoing great changes and major adjustments, which bring new opportunities and challenges to China's development. China's construction of its economy, politics, culture, society, and ecology advance the country, while industrialization, informatization, urbanization and agricultural modernization strengthen and entrench its development. Currently, China is going through an important period as it faces strategic opportunities for further development. The CPC shoulders the heavy responsibilities of promoting reform and opening up, thereby driving the process of socialist modernization in China — a developing country with a population of over one billion. Hence, leading officials at all levels must set a broad world vision and accurately grasp the trends of global development. They should monitor both domestic and international situations, master development initiatives, and enhance their own ability to seize opportunities, whilst addressing risks and challenges. To meet this requirement, they need to continuously update training content, equip officials with the latest theoretical achievements, and educate them on the newest international and domestic situations.

Fourth, establishing a content updating mechanism promotes the growth of officials. The core of the Scientific Outlook on Development is people-oriented, meaning official education and training should center around the needs of trainees, and as a result follow the modern training concept of 'respecting people, serving people, improving people'. Nowadays, officials are generally highly educated, so they have a broad vision and strong sense of democracy and participation, and recognize the different needs of officials in their education and training. The traditional training contents and curriculum cannot meet the needs of officials. Therefore, we need to incessantly update content and courses to adapt to their needs, and set up a mechanism of course development and elimination. Every year, some new courses are offered, and some out-of-date contents are eliminated.

1. Fundamental principles to establish and improve the official education and training content updating mechanism

The first is to follow the laws governing education and training and official growth. The updated official education and training content should be focused on the central tasks of the party and government, so that officials will participate in relevant training and will be equipped with up-to-date knowledge of new policies, business, and new methods. Official education and training institutions should improve the pertinence of official education and training by meticulously designing programs and training courses in accordance with surveys of officials' needs and updating training content accordingly.

The second is to enhance the cultivation of party spirit and emphasize ability training. Leading officials should be educated to remain loyal to the party, and ensure that people outside the party believe in it. The new knowledge, new theories, and new practices should be added to the contents of official education and training to adapt to the increasingly open nature of information in modern society and also to make political theory training more attractive and appealing. In this way, cultivation of party spirit and ability training will be integrated and symbiotic.

The third is to attach importance to basic knowledge education and leadership building. In today's world, as the pace of social economy and informatization increase, the abilities of officials and their training needs also change fast. Therefore, training content should cater to the needs of trainees and add and update the new theories, new knowledge and new skills appropriately.

The fourth is to reinforce the leadership training and the cultivation of comprehensive quality. Official education and training institutions of all types and at all levels should update training contents according to the requirements of the party, the economic and social development of the nation, and changes in the ability and quality of officials, so as to strengthen the relevance of official education and training.

The fifth is to meet the common and individual needs of officials. Compulsory courses are offered to achieve the common objectives of strategic official training tasks. Meanwhile, optional courses are offered to meet the individual needs of trainees, to meet their different capabilities and levels of knowledge. This makes courses more diversified and attractive.

2. Hands-on experience of official education content updating

As a fundamental project for nurturing talent, education and training is emphasized both at home and abroad. Officials have benefited from the rich experiences produced by the updating of training contents and courses.

First, the education and training of officials is oriented towards adapting to changing situations and tasks, and meeting the trainees' needs.

As the party's top university, the Party School of the CPC Central Committee has documented its experiences on the party's central tasks, updating training contents, and playing an important role. In particular, since the implementation of the policy of reform and opening up to the outside world, the university has offered a series of courses on Marxism's principal theories in order to clarify officials' understanding of them. The course that explores the path of socialism with Chinese characteristics informs trainees about the latest achievements in the localization of Marxism in China. In the 21st century, it has equipped officials with great strategic thinking, such as the Scientific Outlook on Development and the concept of building a harmonious socialist society, in line with its teaching contents. The contents arm the minds of trainees, consolidate their belief in following the path of socialism with Chinese characteristics, and improve their ability to promote scientific development and social harmony.

Second, the aim of training is to realize the core tasks and to facilitate core work at any given stage.

Having a central orientation and serving the overall situation are the fundamental requirements of official education and training work. The training should be people-oriented, meeting the needs of officials, and based on leadership building. As a national-level leadership academy, CELAP was built in 2005 to cater to these needs. Since it was founded, CELAP has been carrying out official training by revolving around the center and serving the overall situation. It has primarily formed the 'Pudong model' in official education and training, which is aimed at improving governing capacity, as well as maintaining and developing the party's progressiveness. It takes the spirit of reform and opening up in order to adapt to the current state of global affairs, and following the path of socialism with Chinese characteristics as the teaching focus. The model is characterized by internationalization, contemporaneity and openness. It focuses on improving leadership and governance for the purpose of building a prosperous society in all respects. It also imparts new theories, new knowledge and new practices centered on industrialization, informatization, urbanization and agricultural modernization with Chinese characteristics. CELAP designs teaching and training plans, as well as sequential training themes and programs by taking the themes of building the 'five-in-one' well-off society (building the economy, politics, culture, society and ecological civilization) and the great project of party building. Its training contents focus on new theories, new knowledge and new practices. The teaching tasks are to integrate the latest practice and resources of reform and opening up in the Yangtze River Delta with the resources of the international metropolitan city of Shanghai. It mainly carries out three types of training programs, namely: 'Programs on Urban–rural Integration and Urban Modernization', 'Programs on the International Financial System and Modern Business Management', and 'Programs on New Practices of Reform and Opening up in the Yangtze River Delta'. CELAP has endeavored to make itself the training base for the newest governing methods the exchange base of the latest practice and experience of reform and opening up, the training base for international cooperation in leadership, and the study base of the leadership in urbanization and urban modernization. It plays an important and unique role in international exchange and cooperation. CELAP vigorously carries out international cooperative training. To date, it has trained around 3,200 members from over 120 countries. The training themes concern strengthening the theory and practice of the CPC's governing ability, the successful experiences from 35 years of reform and opening up, leadership cultivation, public administration and China's commercial environment.

Third, updating the content of training and education is based on strengthening surveys of training needs and curriculum development.

For example, CELAP built its curriculum by implementing the functional orientation and school running requirements put forward by the Central Committee, and proposed the training concepts of 'value education, capability building and behavior orientation'. It offers course selection 'menus' and 'modules', and builds the curriculum by focusing on the three themes in the training concept mentioned above. It offers a batch of excellent courses, such as: *Challenges, Opportunities and Solutions to China's Urbanization and Urban Modernization; Urban Governance Innovation and Smart City Construction; The Circular Economy and Low-Carbon Economy in the Yangtze River Delta Region; The Theory and Practice of Building Shanghai into an International Financial Center During the '12th Five-Year Plan' period; Crisis Prevention and Emergency Resolution in Social Management;* and *Public Opinion Guidance in the Period of Social Transformation*. CELAP compiled the *CELAP Collection*, including four volumes, namely, CELAP lecture room, cases, forums and research reports. The first encompasses 30 books, which have been published by People's Publishing House. They are used as the trainees' references and reading materials for autonomous learning, and are highly regarded by officials.

Fourth, the updating of content is driven by implementing teaching evaluation processes and stresses the quality of training.

In China, detailed evaluation questionnaires with detailed scores have been formulated by national-level official schools, such as the Party School of the CPC Central Committee, Chinese Academy of Governance, CELAP, CELAJ and CELAY. After completing the training programs, they evaluate them, form the quality reports and update the courses based on the evaluation results. A section of the province-level party schools implements scientific evaluation on specific courses in practice, and determines whether they need to adjust training content on the basis of the evaluation results.

3. Formulating the teaching content system in line with contemporary requirements

First, we should put more weight on the instruction of socialist theoretical systems with Chinese characteristics, particularly on the Scientific Outlook on Development. Marxist theories lie at the core of China's official education and training system. Marxism is a scientific theory which evolves over time. The theory of socialism with Chinese characteristics is the latest achievement in adapting Marxism to China's conditions, and is the inevitable outcome of the CPC's long-term exploration for truth and a rich harvest of developmental rules. At present, the system of socialist theory with Chinese characteristics should be a focus in the study of Marxist theories in China, and has been given top priority in official education and training, highlighted in their content. The key task of training and teaching this theoretical system is to deepen the study of the Scientific Outlook on Development. Official education and training should take the system of socialist theory with Chinese characteristics and the Scientific Outlook on Development as its principal training content, and work around economic, political, cultural, social and ecological developments with Chinese characteristics as well as important theories and realistic problems in the development of the party to come up with learning themes which help officials gain an in-depth understanding and an overall grasp of the scientific connotations, essence and fundamental requirements of the Scientific Outlook on Development. The efforts taken also aim to correct any misconceptions about the Scientific Outlook on Development, ensure that it is the right path for development and that its policies and measures promote development, and teach officials the mechanism of scientific development so as to apply the theory to economic and social development in general.

Second, we should consistently implement education in party spirit and move it to a more prominent position, especially under current circumstances, so as to enhance the capability of officials to resist corruption and prevent misconduct. The great mission in the education of party spirit is to enable officials at all levels to resist various temptations, keep sober and firm on their political stance, always uphold moral integrity, and behave consistently as disciplined communist members. We should improve this education by integrating lectures, seminars, field study and other methods to enhance the efficacy of teaching on party spirit. We should pay particular attention to teaching of loyalty, to keep officials closely in line with the party, and stay loyal to the party, to the nation, to the people, and to the cause of socialism with Chinese characteristics. We should also conduct teaching on integrity to turn officials into moral examples for the masses with strict self-discipline, and teach them how to resist corruption by adhering to the party's regulations, discipline and constitutional provisions, how to improve their ability to tell right from wrong, how to exert self-control in the face of temptation, and how to remain vigilant against corruption risks by demonstrating typical cases.

Third, we should decide on the content of training and relevant courses oriented to officials themselves and their demands. Being people-oriented lies at the core of the Scientific Outlook on Development, and is an essential value-orientation in official education and training. We should take the overall development of officials as the starting point to carry through their education and training so as to satisfy their needs at different levels. In line with the principle of being people-oriented, training institutions should arrange teaching contents appropriately according to the demands of trainees, and take their learning performance, assessment, feedback, and objective evaluation on teaching quality as important bases for updating courses. Every newly established class should conduct a thorough investigation to identify and integrate post requirements, the individual needs of trainees and the features of the training institution, and then come to work out pertinent teaching content and projects. The institution should design detailed teaching modules with varying characteristics, and endeavor to create a dynamic system of training courses that are updated promptly. The courses should have distinctive themes and features, rich content, and a logical structure, based on a systematic summary of the previous experiences of institutions in developing teaching content and projects, and in accordance with different quality requirements of each training class, training participants and leadership posts.

Fourth, the updating of teaching content and relevant courses should be oriented to cultivating a scientific approach to development. The party and the people are the key forces for the acceleration and stability of economic and social development, and another essential factor is to enhance the capability of officials in conducting a scientific approach to development. The structure of official education and training attempts to guide officials in their study of theory, obtain new knowledge, seek truth, practice party spirit, improve their qualities and abilities, and transform their subjective world. Leading officials should fully acknowledge the importance and urgency of continuous learning in new situations from a strategic point of view, and consider the overall interests of the party and the nation. They should also independently further their own study on the theoretical system of socialism with Chinese characteristics, deepen their understanding of and fully grasp the scientific connotations, spiritual core and essential requirements of the Scientific Outlook on Development, endeavor to keep abreast of the latest achievements of Marxism in China, and conscientiously implement and reinforce the Scientific Outlook on Development with firm resolution. Training institutions should conduct in-depth research into the reinforcement of the Scientific Outlook on Development, as well as the central mission and the general circumstances of different localities and of government institutions. They should strive to then come up with pertinent and pragmatic proposals on the reform of current economic and social development so as to serve the party and the government in scientific decision making while improving the content of official education and training.

Fifth, teaching content and relevant courses should accommodate new trends in economic development, keep up with the times, and ensure that teaching content is contemporary. It has been over 30 years since the launch of the reform and opening-up policy, and China has witnessed fast growth in its own economic, political, cultural, social and economic development. To keep officials updated with the latest knowledge, it is necessary to align the content of teaching as closely as possible with the progression of the times and to make sure that officials have reliable access to information on new trends in economic and social development. Economic globalization involves the whole world, and is a process that speeds up the transmission of risks and turbulence, while shortening the distance between peoples of different countries. We are also aware of how all the nations in the world shift their views on their diplomatic relationships in light of the rise of the PRC. Domestically, we set the transformation of economic development as an innovation-based country, and this should be incorporated into teaching content and relevant courses. The teaching content should also embrace the latest information on economics, politics, science and technology, law, military affairs and social ideology, because official trainees are usually party leaders and need to strengthen their party spirit, constantly renew and enrich their command of theory and knowledge, and enhance their leadership capacity.

Sixth, we should endeavor to raise our level of research in order to consolidate the foundation for updating teaching content and relevant courses. High-quality teaching is grounded on in-depth research, which functions as the prerequisite for developing new courses and disposing of those that are obsolete. Integrating closely with the current features of China's economic and social development, training institutions of all levels should conduct research on important missions and difficulties in local economic and social development during the process of reform and opening up, and should investigate into critical issues and key problems that party leaders are most concerned with and willing to resolve. We should cultivate a competent and reliable research and teaching faculty, supply them with sufficient funds, and forge a mutually reciprocal relationship between research and teaching. In order to do this we must carry out research regarding teaching themes while using research results to improve teaching, and eventually create favorable teaching conditions by pooling and integrating achievements in both teaching and research in the classroom.

Chapter 3

How to Learn

Following the introduction to the content of official education and training, we will explore the educational modules and training methods.

I. Educational Modules

The *Regulations on Official Education and Training Work (Trial)* stipulates the time frame and the way in which officials participate in education and training. According to the Regulations, the CPC and leading government officials at the levels of province, ministry, bureau, city and county should participate, for at least three months every five years, in the training programs provided by party schools, schools of administration, leadership academies, or training institutions accredited by relevant personnel departments above the city and bureau levels. Officials who are promoted, but have not received official education nor met the requirements set by training institutions due to exceptional circumstances, should complete the education and training within one year after their promotion. Eight hours of academic training each day is the standard. *Suggestions on the 2008-2012 Implementation of Large-scale Official Training Work* converts the time frame of training in accordance with the requirement prescribed by the *Regulations on Official Education and Training Work (Trial)* into no less than 110 academic hours each year, and cumulatively up to 550 hours every five years for officials at province, ministry, bureau, city and county levels.

For officials at and below the prefectural level, the *Regulations* stipulates that they should spend no less than 12 days each year in total on full-time training, or 100 academic hours calculated in accordance with the standard of eight hours of class each day.

1. The training can be classified into four types, depending on the content.

The *Regulations on Official Education and Training Work (Trial)* divides the four types of official education and training into: various on-the-job training, promotion-oriented training, specialized professional training for specific posts, and orientation training for the newly employed.

On-the-job training is organized to meet the needs of officials as they carry out their duties during the occupancy of their post, and includes political theory, policies, laws and regulations, professional knowledge, culture and skills. On-the-job training comes first in official education and training, and upholds the principle of 'learning for what one is doing, and providing what one is lacking', in that it meets the requirements of social development and the professional demands of officials at different levels. On-the-job training attaches great importance to the education and training of new theories, new knowledge and new skills, and designs different training programs with varied content, which officials can choose from in accordance with what they want to learn and what they need for their job qualifications. In so doing, officials are better motivated to participate in their education and training, and the efficacy and pertinence of the education and training is improved.

Promotion-oriented training is implemented for officials who are to be promoted to a leading post. It is generally carried out before the officials take office. If the personnel department in charge of appointment and dismissal permits, officials can also participate in the training within one year after their promotion. This type of training focuses on policies and theories, specialized professional knowledge, and organizing and leading capabilities, which the officials are in great need of when they take their posts, and with which they will better fulfill their new duties. Promotion-oriented training should be implemented hierarchically relevant to their administrative power.

Specialized professional training focuses on the knowledge, skills and methods that officials need when they are engaged in their specific work. The actual time, content and methods should be determined by the practical demands of the specific work. Specialized training can be held in the form of full-time training classes to ensure that officials are competent at their post.

Orientation training is arranged for newly appointed officials during the probationary period. It mainly covers basic knowledge for the position, working procedures and methods. It can be organized in the form of training classes or work-based study. The newly appointed officials can therefore develop a clear understanding of the characteristics and procedures of their new positions, as well as of the organizational disciplines, professional ethics, and their work scope and responsibilities. By taking the training, officials acquire the qualifications required for their new positions and improve their overall competence.

2. Training methods can be divided into the following types:

The Party Committee (leading party group) Central Group Learning is an important method of on-the-job training for leading groups and officials at different levels. On-the-job training is a vital measure in enhancing the ideological and political development of officials at different levels, and an important channel to improve the CPC's governing capacity and develop a study-oriented party. The Party Committee (leading party group) Central Group Learning was initiated in some provincial party committees in the 1980s, and it was gradually institutionalized after the 14th National Congress of the CPC. In September, 2009 the Organization Department of the CPC Central Committee and the Publicity Department of the CPC Central Committee issued *Opinions on Strengthening and Improving the Party Committee (Leading Party Group) Central Group Learning*, which stipulates in detail the significance, objectives, content, learning style and systems of the Party Committee (leading party group) Central Group Learning. The *Opinions* explicitly takes the in-depth study and implementation of the socialist theoretical system with Chinese characteristics as the primary task, with the mastering and application of the Marxist viewpoint and methods as the fundamental objective, and routine group study and discussion as the main learning form of the Central Group Learning. The routine group study should not occur less than once every quarter of a year, and the secretary of the Party Committee (leading party group) is the first person responsible for the Central Group Learning. The main duty of the Party Committee Organization Department is to coordinate with the Publicity Department in intensifying the guidance service, supervision and inspection, and to carry out an evaluation of the Central Group Learning.

Case 2 Routine Group Study of the Political Bureau of the Central Committee

The Political Bureau of the CPC Central Committee is elected at the plenary session of the CPC Central Committee. A member of the Political Bureau of the CPC Central Committee is known as a Member of the Political Bureau of the Central Committee, or Member of the Political Bureau. The Political Bureau of the CPC and its Standing Committee exercise the functions and powers of the Central Committee when the Central Committee is not in session. The routine group study among members of the Political Bureau of the CPC is a significant and important system innovation. From 2002, when the 16th CPC National Congress was held, until 2012 before the 18th CPC National Congress, the Political Bureau of the Central Committee undertook their routine group study 77 times (44 times after the 16th CPC National Congress, 33 times after the 17th CPC National Congress). The topics of the routine group study focus on key points, critical current issues, and difficulties in the governance, administration and modernization of the CPC. The content covers major issues on the economy, legal system, military affairs, science and technology, culture, education, healthcare, employment and social welfare. Routine group study is carried out by the General Office of the Central Committee, relevant ministries and relevant research institutions, together in collaboration. The General Office of the Central Committee takes the lead and the Central Policy Research Office is in charge of topic selection. The General Secretary of the CPC chairs each session. First, specialists and scholars expound a significant problem; the members then discuss and exchange their ideas, and finally the General Secretary delivers a summary speech. The institutionalized routine group study of the Political Bureau of the Central Committee is of exemplary significance to the theoretical study of party committees at different levels, the construction of a leading group, and the cultivation of capabilities.

Organizational training is where the administration department of official education and training transfers officials, based on their needs and the requirements of their positions, to specified education and training institutions to participate in full-time learning. At present, as a main form of official education and training, organizational training is required for training in political theory, education on the nature of the party, and significant strategic plans of the state and party. Organizational training has three characteristics: obligatory participation, fixed training time and uniformity of training content. Its merits include powerful organizational planning, scientific and reasonable control and arrangement to cater to the scale, level, quality, and effectiveness of official education and training. There are, however, disadvantages. Organizational training delivers mainly top-down mandates, so most trainees lack motivation and complete the tasks passively. Training content is not trainee-oriented as they are unable to solve the urgent and practical problems officials face. In particular, since the Central Committee demanded large-scale official training and large-scale improvement of the quality of officials, they have become less and less sufficient to meet the requirements of new situations. The problems are paradoxically that some officials participate in more training than needed, while others take no training at all. Currently, there are three types of centralized full-time training during which officials leave their work and job sites. The first is the hierarchical full-time education and training for officials at different levels. It emphasizes the trainees' position and level, and is aimed at improving their initiative and capability when they embark on their new position. It meets the requisite knowledge, skills and attitude of the position, and provides standardized training based on the prescribed teaching methods. It is characterized by periodic training. The second is the classified full-time training for different positions. It stresses professionalism, flexibility and opportunism. The third is staging full-time training according to the experience of officials, for instance, promotion-oriented training before or after taking office; orientation training early in the tenure, and regular or irregular training along with promotion.

Self-selection learning means that officials, under the guidance of the administration department in charge of official education and training, choose their training methods in accordance with their training needs. This is an innovative move stemming from the practice of large-scale official training in various regions. It also represents the Scientific Outlook on Development in the practice of official education and training, and supplements organizational training. Self-selection learning differs from organizational training in the following respects: First, officials autonomously determine whether they will apply for training. Second is its selectivity: the training takes the form of menus, such as a curriculum menu, training institutions menu, and training teachers menu. Third is that it is market-oriented. Marketing measures are adopted to integrate social educational resources with the service of official education and training. Self-selection learning is an open and personalized training mode, conforming to the general rules of official education and training. The official education and training administration department formulates the relevant management system, and establishes the scope of officials, institutions and the contents of self-selection learning. The institutions for self-selection learning regularly publicize their menus and specific arrangements, and provide favorable learning conditions and environments for participating officials. There are, however, issues with self-selection learning: First, it is hard to supervise. Second, regarding the platform for self-selection learning, the quality of the training resources is not adequate. In most regions, the training base and network are not yet set up with reasonable arrangements, complete range and functions, and advantages which complement each other.

On-the-job self-taught training means that officials do not leave work and participate in routine group study organized by institutions, but teach themselves to meet the requirements of their positions during their work or in their spare time. Their institutions should urge the officials to improve their work competence and to take on-the-job training. The institutions should also encourage the officials to carry through lifelong learning and learning while working, and should provide them with sufficient conditions to do so. The officials can take various forms of learning, and form different learning groups. On-the-job self-taught learning should be closely integrated with the demands of the work at hand. It focuses on the socialist theoretical system with Chinese characteristics, knowledge of the socialist market economy, laws and regulations, modern management, modern science and technology, history, literature and art. It is aimed at integrating various types of knowledge with the solutions to their practical problems in order to improve their working ability and innovating capability.

Centralized refresher training refers to a type of theme-oriented updating training during which arrangements are made for a group of officials from a certain department or of a certain level to attend certain institutions in order to learn a specific, emerging topic or to meet certain construction tasks in a given period. It helps officials reach consensus, build mutual understanding, and cooperate to promote their work effectively. The duration is generally about one month, and is carried out in the form of full-time or part-time training. In recent years, officials above the county or division level have taken centralized refresher training on the theme of the Scientific Outlook on Development.

Theme training focuses on particular subjects that are closely related to the central task of economic and social development, and the training content is aimed at resolving difficulties and problems related to this task. Theme training therefore serves the overall interest of the nation, and must be pertinent and effective in doing so. Trainees are selected according to officials' categorization and work specialization. The training methods involve lectures held by experts, teaching the interpretations of leaders, learners' discussions and on-the-spot teaching. After the theme training, a report which provides reference for specific subject solutions with certain decisions must be released. Since the 17th Congress of the CPC, departments and training institutions in different regions have enhanced the training to solve difficulties and key issues in economic and social development, focusing on specific subjects such as urbanization, independent innovation, guaranteeing people's livelihood, crisis response systems and innovation in social administration. This type of training has contributed significantly to solving problems raised by economic and social development.

Network-based training is an extension of self-selection learning. It is a learner-oriented, non-traditional type of education based on usage of the internet. It has the advantages of fast information dissemination, rich resources, temporal and spatial flexibility, is low in cost, and it provides officials with the choice of self-selection learning which is characterized by 'compatibility, openness and sharing'. Meanwhile, network-based learning provides a platform for the effective combination of organizational training and self-selection learning. It enables officials to take certain courses at a given time through the platform, and to take self-selection learning whenever and wherever possible. It takes into account the practical situation of their positions so they can complete the required hours and credits in order to achieve effects similar to organizational training. Network-based learning has the following three characteristics. The first is the abundance of network learning resources that is shared. The second is taking the individual's autonomous and collaborative learning combined as the major learning form. The third is that it goes beyond the temporal and spatial limitations of traditional learning methods. Currently, a large number of official training institutions take advantage of the advanced and convenient network system and its abundant teaching and training resources to further develop network learning and distance training. For instance, at the national level, the Organization Department of the CPC Central Committee has built China's official network institutes; at the level of training institutions, the Party School of the CPC Central Committee has set up its distance education network. CELAP has established its online learning platform. In addition, a number of provinces have built official online learning systems and online colleges.

Case 3 Network College of CELAP

The Network College of CELAP is a subordinate institution to CELAP, collaborating with the Department of Information and Technology. Under the guidance of the *Regulations on Official Education and Training Work (Trial)* and the *Reform Program for Official Education and Training from 2010 to 2020*, and in the spirit of national official education, the Network College takes full advantage of the abundant teaching resources of CELAP, carefully designs the curricula to strengthen the thinking and beliefs of officials, to improve their governing capability and leading competence as the key teaching points, and strives to provide educational training on different themes for party and government officials at different levels.

Regarding the teaching methods, it adopts web-based learning which is supplemented with experts' instructions, answers to questions, live online interactions, and on-the-spot teaching in the developed Yangtze River Delta. It employs both network background management and organization field management, supervising and assessing the learners' web-based training. Learning content includes obligatory and optional courses, catering to the demands of the party and the nation, while meeting the individual needs and diversity of officials. The Network College offers its official education and training resources with a flexible learning timetable, rich course content, diversified instruction forms, first-rate training, and low costs. It mediates the conflicts between the work and study of officials, and enhances the pertinence and effectiveness of official education and training, playing a significant role in fully implementing the strategic task of large-scale official training.

Teaching Modules:

1. Network Theme Class (supplemented with information-based means such as live online lectures and a Q & A session)

2. 'Network and Field-work Investigation' Theme Class (combined with on-the-spot teaching on the main campus and the Yangtze River Delta)

3. Online Learning (logging into the College's online learning platform key, and then learning freely)

Teaching Management:

1. Curriculum design: The curriculum reflects the needs of both the client department and their officials. Based on the theme training courses, the curriculum is redesigned in accordance with the principle of consensus. The curriculum includes obligatory and optional courses.

2. Training methods: Online learning is supplemented by live online

interaction, experts' instructions, and the on-the-spot teaching in the Yangtze River Delta.

3. Duration of training: Theme classes generally last three months, and fundamental learning classes one year.

4. Participant management: Network monitoring management and organizational management are adopted to supervise and assess participants' online learning. After they complete the set credit hours, trainees can take the online tests or submit the summary report to gain credits. After the completion of the required learning hours and credits, participants are granted graduation permission and are awarded the Graduate Certificate of the Network College of CELAP.

5. Extended service: After graduation from the Network College, trainees can continue to use the resources of the Network College of CELAP for a prolonged period of time, with access to information and to some courses via the information pushing system.

The Network College is ahead of others in its exploration of quality resources to serve the grassroots level. Guided by the principle of being 'oriented to organizational needs, centered on theme training, and focused on the grassroots level', the Network College collaborates with organization departments and party schools in different regions, laying emphasis on the choice of training themes and trainee management during the whole training process. It combines the teaching resources of CELAP with courses with local characteristics, and integrates online learning courses and face-to-face teaching available to those at the grassroots level, who have few training opportunities but need to improve their capabilities and expand their belief in the party spirit. While providing the grassroots-level officials with personalized network training in the form of a 'nutrition formula to suit their training diet', the Network College takes trainees to the red revolutionary memorial halls and the on-the-spot teaching bases in the Yangtze River Delta to learn through experience and investigation. This is organized to further explore 'network and on-the-spot' training modules and to enhance the appeal and attractiveness of the program to officials. In March 2011, the Network College together with the Organization Department of Chengdu Municipal Party Committee

set up the Chengdu network teaching base of CELAP. It also worked with the Organization Department of Haidong Prefectural Party Committee in Qinghai to set up its second network teaching base. Network teaching bases have gradually become the 'strongholds' of knowledge and serve the grassroots officials. After over two years of exploration and practice, the Network College, along with organization departments and party schools in various regions and cities, has trained over 30,000 grassroots officials. The training has generated a positive response from trainees, demonstrating the benefits of this training method in serving local party committees and local governments.

Training by serving in a temporary position is when officials are sent to work in new positions and experience new working environments. Before serving in a temporary position, the officials are gathered to take an orientation course and are provided with the necessary knowledge and introduction to their new situations. While serving in a temporary position, officials participate in training constantly to improve their work capability, depending on the requirements of their positions. At the end of their service, arrangements are also made for officials to take a final training session as a summary to further improve their ability.

Officials undergo sectional training according to prescribed requirements, such as adopting different training modules in various forms and in different training institutions. Sectional training should be designed to center on training objectives and stress rational transitions between sections. In accordance with the requirements of the Central Committee leaders, official colleges at the national level should strive to structure training so that it has distinct advantages, complementary features and complete functions, and thereby forms a training chain with organic connections. For example, after offering theories and knowledge for a certain period of time, the Party School of the CPC Central Committee will send some classes to CELAJ, to be educated on party spirit by making use of the rich local red resources. This takes advantage of various colleges and increases the overall efficacy of official education and training.

Personalized training offers tailored training plans and courses to officials in terms of the requirements of the corresponding responsibilities of their positions, their individual competence and requirements of their career development. It is therefore both people-oriented and need-oriented. The training plan is centered on officials, a feature which represents the modernization of official education and training.

3. Developing new training patterns by combining organizational training and self-selection training

Despite there being many forms of official training, the major two training patterns are organizational training and self-selection training. Organizational training is the training system in which officials are transferred to specific training institutions to participate in full-time learning. Official self-selection learning is where officials independently choose their modes of training according to their own needs. With further reform of official education and training, the relations between them must be properly handled so that the integrated training pattern can be further developed.

We must first pinpoint the objectives of integrated training. Only by integrating organizational training and self-selection learning can the needs of officials, as well as the positions and responsibilities of their posts, be met and achieved in a real sense. Where organizational training is employed to meet the requirements of organizations and the positions of officials, self-selection training adheres to the training concept of lifelong learning, and is adopted to meet the needs of the officials in their personal development, and to resolve the conflicts between what they want to learn and what they are required to learn. When integrating organizational training and self-selection learning, the content design of self-selection learning puts particular emphasis on enhancing operational capacity on the basis of the CPC's demands on official education and training in the new era, to further improve the cultural and scientific quality of officials, as well as their ability to use their knowledge to solve new problems. In terms of the training methods, personalized official training plans are formulated based on the varying learning needs of officials. Organizational training should represent the emphasis of 'theoretical and party spirit education' in official education and training, while self-selection learning puts more stress on the improvement of ability and enabling officials to better serve scientific development.

The second point is to carry forward the integration of the two training patterns. The process of self-selection should be fully reflected in organizational training. For instance, the training themes, timetables, contents and methods are determined in accordance with feedback from surveys on the training needs of officials. Suitable and diversified training methods are employed after fully understanding the opinions and requirements and widely solicited ideas of trainees.

The organizational intentions are fully reflected in the official self-selection training. In the designing of training themes and the curriculum, both the individual preferences of officials and the organizations' demands of them are taken into consideration. The department in charge of official education and training offers theoretical knowledge concerning party spirit and theory based on the requirements of the situations and tasks. The evaluation system of self-selection learning is set up to gauge whether trainees have met the requirements or have achieved the desired effects as a result of the training. Those who have failed to meet the requirements will be penalized. Only by operating along with the learning evaluation system can self-selection learning achieve its desired effects and expected goals.

The third point is to construct a system to guarantee the integration of the two training patterns. First, the training market is established and improved for the rational allocation of training resources. According to the requirement of constructing a system of training institutions characterized by 'clear-cut work division, complementary advantages, rational layout, and orderly competition', as stated in the *Regulations on Official Education and Training Work (Trial)*, the educational resources are further integrated by means of market-based project bidding. Redundant training is removed. A teachers' database system has been set up for the training bases to share resources. The orderly market permit system and scientific evaluation system have been set up. Training institutions of various types are evaluated regularly to determine the qualification levels of the training providers, in order to ensure that the training institutions can enjoy fair access and competition. The quality of the training is checked and evaluated at regular intervals to measure whether the training plan is feasible and logical, whether the training content is pertinent, whether the training methods match the training content, and whether the teachers are aptly qualified. In so doing, the evaluation encourages the development and standardization of the system.

Second, the management system is established and improved. A uniform registration system of official education and training is practiced. By means of modern information technology, the self-contained management system of the electronic files of official education and training is set up. A file is created for each official participating in the training, and is handed down to each training institution, which accurately documents the training record of the official. This provides a multi-dimensional and full track record of the training undertaken by each official. The class hour monitoring system is used. The overall training process is monitored by the relevant indexes of both learning quantity and quality to guarantee the overall quality of education and training.

Third, self-selection training is extended. As time goes by, solely conducting organizational training cannot keep up with the personal development and diversified work requirements of officials, so we should continuously extend the official self-selection learning pattern. For example, the official online learning platform is a self-selection learning management system which integrates the network selection of officials with learning content, learning time, class hour statistics, learning management and tests. This learning platform enables trainees to enjoy richer learning content and more freedom in terms of when and where they learn, so as to meet the requirements of officials of various sectors, types and levels. The extended self-selection learning pattern facilitates the combination of organizational training and self-selection learning, ensuring the accomplishment of large-scale official training tasks.

II. Teaching Methods

Good teaching methods not only impart theory and knowledge accurately, vividly and effectively, but also facilitate learning initiative and creativity in trainees. In recent years, the variety of teaching methods has been increasing. Besides lectures, research-based teaching, case studies, simulation and experiential training, there is active learning, interactive teaching, lab-based teaching and structured workshops. The diversified teaching methods may overlap and be integrated with each other.

1. Lecture-based teaching method

This is a basic teaching method in official education and training. Teachers, according to the learners' cognitive rules, organize and control the teaching process purposefully in a planned way, enabling learners to master the basic knowledge and skills systematically. The advantage of this method is that teachers fully utilize their leading role. Teachers can teach a large number of learners simultaneously, and learners can learn a significant amount of information in a given time. There are two sources for lecturers. One is the experts and scholars working at the official training institutions, who specialize in systematic theoretical learning and research on current issues. The other is inviting officials and scholars both from home and abroad to give lectures. For example, CELAP, which has both 'officials teaching and teaching officials', invites policy makers, policy interpreters, and policy executors to give lectures and in doing so achieves favorable training results. In order to stimulate initiative and enthusiasm in learning, many schools prioritize interaction in lectures, leaving adequate time for teachers to answer learners' questions and for further discussion. Through this interaction, both teachers and students benefit and draw inspiration from each other.

2. Experiential teaching

On-the-spot teaching and scenario simulation are the two methods most frequently used in experiential teaching.

On-the-spot teaching is one of the experiential teaching methods widely applied by various leadership training institutions. In order to facilitate the connection of theory with practice in the minds of trainees, institutions send them to grassroots-level work units, offices and enterprises to undergo on-

Students of China Jinggangshan Cadre Academy in Red Army uniform at a class at Longjiang Academy (Qianyi, Xinhua News Agency)

the-spot teaching, with sites of economic and social development as training classrooms, the materials in practice as training content, and front-line workers as teachers. This method guides trainees to integrate theory with practice, and improves their ability to do so. On-the-spot teaching generally includes introductions to background information, field trip experience, discussion and exchange, teachers' comments, and research report writing. CELAP has progressively explored the on-the-spot teaching method, and has accumulated certain results from training experiences. On-the-spot teaching is carried out in three forms. The first is social investigation. Current issues and difficult problems as identified by trainees are listed as the investigation subjects, and then CELAP organizes the trainees to carry out the investigation. For instance, trainees went to Kunshan in Jiangsu Province to carry out investigations on the theme of balancing urban and rural development and to conduct field study activities. The second is to implement on-the-spot teaching with special subjects step by step. For example, during the Shanghai World Expo, CELAP first invited the Expo officials to explain the Expo theme of 'Better City, Better Life', and then sent trainees to the Urban Best Practices Area of the World Expo to visit and observe the practices of each city. The third is social study. CELAP has developed over 260 field study sites, offering more than 600 courses, and founded Kunshan College, boosting the development of on-the-spot teaching or field research.

Scenario simulation teaching: in this method, workshop scenarios are set up in the classroom with learners playing different roles. By role-playing, learners experience the working conditions and feel of the roles they are playing, while exercising their skills and gathering experience for the work they will engage in.

> **Case 4 The Implementation of Experiential Teaching by CELAP**
>
> CELAP lays emphasis on experiential teaching. It took the lead in constructing six theme laboratories. These are the media and communications lab, the crisis management lab, the psychological adjustment lab, the financial transaction lab, the 'smart city' lab and the party building lab. Using the theme laboratories, CELAP constantly develops characteristic training courses to meet the needs of officials at intermediate and senior levels.

Students of CELAP at a training class on how to handle public hazards (Ren Long, Xinhua News Agency)

Case 5 Implementation of the Immersion Learning Program by the National Defense University (NDU)

The development and wide application of information technology not only triggered profound changes in each social sector, but also brought about a revolution in learning. Immersion learning simulates and emulates the real world, and even produces better effects than the actual environment, making immersion a vital element to motivate learning, cultivate learning interest, and develop learning initiative and creativity. The NDU has taken beneficial steps in immersion teaching, and formulated Immersive Seminar Gaming, a new training method that emphasizes virtual scenarios and environments based on modern warfare simulation technology. Its key feature is to build a virtual time and space, and strategic decision-making environment close to actual situations by means of the integrated application of the methods of role-play, environmental cues, process simulation, and responsive feedback. It enables the participants to access intelligence, make strategic decisions, organize and implement strategic moves, incur strategy evolution via multiple interactions, give prompt feedback and adjust their decisions on a timely basis, and shoulder the responsibility for the success or failure of their decisions. This method creates a strong sense of environment immersion, role immersion and process immersion, enabling the participants to gain strategic decision-making experience during their training.

3. Case teaching

The features of case teaching are research, simulation and experiential teaching. The effect of case teaching mainly depends on the applicability of selected cases. Good cases should be applicable, serve certain teaching objectives and cover the teaching contents, so as to tactfully integrate basic concepts, principal theories, methods of analysis, and decision-making skills. Meanwhile, the cases should be relevant to the thoughts and life of the trainees, and the selected foreign cases should be incorporated with local conditions. The teaching process is centered on the learner and guided by the teacher, who leads the learners to reflect on, debate on, choose and make decisions on specific and critical issues in the case study. There are two basic models in case teaching. One is knowledge-oriented, expounding fundamental principles with cases. The other is competency-oriented, aimed at improving the competence of trainees in making policies, enforcing policies, and accomplishing certain tasks.

4. Research-based teaching

As a method centered around problems, research-based teaching focuses on reform in the current training institutions. Research-based teaching is where trainees conduct research on certain subjects under the guidance of the teachers, and acquire knowledge from research on their own initiative. A large number of colleges proposed the project with features that are 'problem-oriented and targeted at competency'. This teaching method attaches great importance to practical work, and problems in their work are often brought to the classroom to seek a solution. The learning objectives are to apply and solve problems. It focuses on group discussion and group research as the learning process. The training outcomes are presented in the form of work improvement proposals, drafts of important documents and research reports. This learning method fully encourages the growth of each trainee's initiative and creativity through the research experience, and proves the distinctive advantage of the group research method over individual wisdom and experience.

5. Action Learning

The British scholar and professor Reg Revans pioneered Action Learning in 1965 as an approach to train managerial staff. The fundamental concepts are as follows. Learning cannot be separated from practice. Experienced managers do not read and then apply what they have learned to practice, but learn by doing. The next is the basic procedure. A set of managers determine problems designed and organized by their trainers which they expect to resolve in practice on their own. They meet for one day on a regular basis and exchange ideas on or reflect on the problems to be tackled. They encourage each other, form development programs to solve problems, and then return to their posts, putting the established work program into practice. Meanwhile, they continue identifying problems, gaining new experiences and meeting regularly to partake in learning, reflecting on and discussing activities until they reach agreement on the work procedure for the next development stage. They have to work through several cycles before they eventually resolve a specific problem. A prolonged Action Learning project may last over a year.

> **Case 6 The Implementation of Action Learning by the National Organization and Official Institute**
>
> In the early 1990s, the Action Learning method started to draw the attention of some Chinese training institutions. The National Organization and Official Institute of the Organization Department of the CPC Central Committee introduced the new training model with Action Learning through its international cooperative training program, and adopted the concept of 'learning by doing and doing while learning drives thinking and facilitates solutions to problems, and eventually enhances development' as its core. The institute focused on certain key challenges concerning local economic and social development, organized a cross-sector core personnel department to make up a team, and adopted the systematic learning methods, which include investigating problems, centralized training and discussion, rectifying working practices, overseas comparative study and exploring solutions. The institute assists the local organization departments to improve the thinking of officials by solving practical problems. It has carried out the program by fostering a team of qualified officials in provinces and cities such as Gansu, Qinghai, Inner Mongolia, Sichuan, Guangxi, Chongqing, Hainan, Jiangsu and Jiangxi, effectively boosting local development.

6. Hands-on learning

Some official training institutions organize trainees to go to rural areas, factories and military bases to work as farmers, workers or soldiers for a period of time in order to understand the grassroots work, to experience life, to strengthen their will and to improve their work capacity. Some official training institutions direct trainees to carry out investigations and study certain problems to gain an understanding of the conditions of the nation, province, city, county, town, village as well as the people. They learn and improve by implementing investigations and studies to help and solve problems for the masses, submit investigation reports and learning summaries, and put forward advisory opinions and suggestions on leadership decision-making.

7. Structured workshops

As a new training method, in recent years, structured workshops have been widely adopted in training classrooms at official training institutions. The structured workshops have important theoretical and practical value for the innovation of official training. Centering on a theme that participants are concerned about and guided by the training facilitators, a structured workshop follows certain procedures and rules, and trainees carry out research from different perspectives step by step, learning and developing their decision-making skills as a group. The structured workshop has the following characteristics. First, researched topics are structured. The topics themselves are usually generated by trainees. The trainees must solve practical problems regarding the topics. In practice, the training institutions collect the problems generated by the trainees and comb through them to formulate them into several topics, which then will be presented as key problems during the training. Then the institutions determine the theme in the final seminar in a democratic way, which the trainees then proceed to work on in the workshop. During this process, the facilitators determine the subtopics for each period based on the overall theme, including problems, causes, and possible solutions. Once the subtopics are determined, the facilitators will intentionally lead trainees to work on the subtopics step by step. The process by which the institutions determine the theme ensures that the topics for discussion are logically structured, well arranged, and conducive to active participation.

Second, members of structured workshops are made up of facilitators and trainees. The members are classified into several groups according to certain rules, and each group is accompanied by a facilitator. The function of the facilitator is to ensure that trainees think and communicate in a more effective way. Besides the targeted knowledge content, the facilitator pays attention to fostering good ways of thinking and talking to the trainees. A facilitator is often an external training expert to guarantee neutrality and objectivity, so that they can win trust from participants. The grouping of the workshop members is formed through a combination of the independent choice of the trainees and the arrangement of class advisors. Once the members of each group are arranged, the members cannot change groups throughout the workshop (which generally lasts three to five days) without permission.

Third, the workshop procedure is structured. A structured workshop generally consists of four stages. At the first stage, topics to be discussed are organized democratically. At the second stage, under the guidance of the facilitator, participants carry out a three-phase workshop centered on a theme. At the third stage, a representative of the group presents to the whole class, and teachers and experts comment on it. At the fourth stage, participants deepen their understanding, come up with new ideas and write a research report. The second stage includes three steps: selecting problems and defining the concepts, analyzing phenomena and investigating the crucial factors and reasons, and finally proposing suggestions and forming a feasible program. The staged and structured workshop requires participants to slow down their pace of thinking and carry out investigations by strictly following the discussion and requirements for each topic. The procedure of the structured workshop ensures that the phasing of each stage is followed. To maximize training results, the participants must prepare before class.

Fourth, the methods of assessment for the workshops are structured. Experienced training institutions should scientifically design assessments to measure training outcomes and the participants' learning, and evaluate the training effects from the perspectives of both teacher and learner, so that they can gradually improve the training standard and quality. The structured workshop theme and procedure allow the full-time teaching and research departments to formulate assessments in advance, to review each workshop topic through discussion, and to supervise each stage, so that the assessment results will be more objective, fair and valuable. At the same time, during a structured workshop, each group can form a research report relevant to the required topic based on their discussion and communication. The research reports are submitted by the facilitator to experts in the research field for scientific assessment and the results are returned to the participants, allowing the latter to further assess the group members' research and to recognize their own achievements and setbacks in the workshop, increasing the efficacy of the assessment mechanism.

8. Integrated teaching

CELAP developed the integrated teaching method by drawing on advanced training experiences both at home and abroad. Integrated teaching methods include integrated workshops, integrated case teaching, and integrated classroom lectures. The integrated workshop combines class themes and the characteristics of participants, encouraging them to select different discussion topics in accordance with their interests, and thereby increasing their enthusiasm for learning. In such a way, each participant can express and exchange opinions on a topic, analyze its causes and discuss solutions to its problems. This can both increase trainees' participation and make the topics more relevant as the discussion will not just focus on superficial problems. Participants can also propose detailed solutions and deepen teaching research. With the multi-case integrated method, several leading officials with practical experience are invited to introduce cases to trainees to help them broaden their horizons and to make case teaching more representative and diversified.

> **Case 7 The Implementation of Integrated Teaching by CELAP**
>
> CELAP launched a workshop with the theme of urban community grassroots party organization and construction, and offered teaching centered on 'the innovative practice of urban community construction'. CELAP invited the Deputy Minister of the Dalian Municipal Organization Department and the Director of Wuhan City Baibuting Community Management Committee to introduce their local conditions of the community party construction. Integrated teaching focuses on themes from many different perspectives. In the workshop with the theme of economic and social development in the western regions, CELAP invited practitioners from the western regions, decision-makers of the central ministries, as well as scholars and foreign experts to give lessons to the workshop members, each analyzing the western regions from a different perspective. The Vice Governor of Guizhou province spoke about the development of the western region at the province level. The teaching content is based on reality, theory and relevance. The chief planner of the Ministry of Transportation and officials from the National Emergency Office spoke on the development of the western region from the perspective of the Central Committee. The integrated media course offered by foreign media experts enabled participants to gain an overall understanding of overseas views on western regional development. Participants very much appreciated this integrated teaching method.

Chapter 4

Where to Learn

CELAP, CELAJ and CELAY were established with the approval of the CPC Central Committee and the State Council, and are directed by the Organization Department of the CPC Central Committee. They held their completion and opening ceremonies simultaneously in March 2005. The minister of the Organization Department of the CPC Central Committee is the president of all three executive leadership academies.

Under the guidance of a leading educational department, institutions are responsible for concrete training tasks and the implementation of official education and training. In order to further improve official education and training we must enhance these institutions.

We attach great importance to the construction of official education and training institutions. The CPC built official education and training institutions to cater to emerging work demands during the different periods of national revolution, construction and reform and development. The CPC set up peasant movement institutes in the early period, Red Army Officer Training Corps in the Jinggangshan period, and the Party School of the CPC Central Committee, the Anti-Japanese Military and Political University, and public schools in Northern Shaanxi during the Yan'an period. Since 1949 when the PRC was founded, and particularly since the Third Plenary Session of the 11th Central Committee of the CPC, the CPC has made significant progress in the construction of official education and training institutions, and has formed a relatively complete system of local party schools and schools of administration. Fully developed departments and professional official education and training institutions have been established with a new layout at the national level composed of the Party School of the CPC Central Committee, the Chinese Academy of Governance, CELAP, CELAJ, and CELAY.

I. System of Training Institutions

After years of practice, China has built a sophisticated network of training institutions of different administrative levels. Besides official education and training institutions at the national level, each province, city and county now has its local party school.

From a vertical point of view, the national-level training institutions include the Party School of the CPC Central Committee, the Chinese Academy of Governance, and CELAP, CELAJ and CELAY. Each province (autonomous region, municipality), city (region, autonomous prefecture, league), and county (town, district, banner) has also built its corresponding school of administration or party school.

From a horizontal perspective, China's official education and training institutions mainly include party schools, schools of administration, leadership academies, professional training institutions, and official training

	Party school	School of administration	Leadership academy
National level	Party School of the CPC Central Committee	Chinese Academy of Governance	CELAP, CELAJ, CELAY
Province (autonomous region, municipality)	Party school in each province (autonomous region, municipality)	School of administration in each province (autonomous region, municipality)	Utilizing unique training resources and building leadership academies at different levels
City (prefecture, autonomous prefecture, league)	Party school in each city (region autonomous prefecture, league)	School of administration in each city (region, autonomous prefecture, league)	
County (town, district, banner)	Party school in each county (town, district, banner)	School of administration in each county (town, district, banner)	

bases in institutions of higher learning. In addition, teaching and research bases for practice are developed according to actual needs, and collaborations are forged with overseas universities and other training providers to further develop China's official education and training programs.

There are also virtual training bases, such as network institutes and online learning platforms. The diversified official education and training institutions at different levels respectively fulfill their training functions and take on their corresponding tasks.

1. Classification and management of official education and training institutions

In China, the Official Education Bureau of the Organization Department of the CPC Central Committee is responsible for the management of official education and training nationwide. Different types of official education and training institutions at different levels operate under the guidance and management of the Official Education Bureau of the Organization Department of the CPC Central Committee. Generally speaking, the Official Education Bureau provides macro-management for official training institutions of all types at different levels and sets the principles for the running of the schools, but it does not intervene in their operations directly. Training institutions of all types are under direct management of their relevant department in their own system, and operate under the guidance of a superior department.

The party school system is under the leadership of party committees. The party school is one of the departments of the party committee. Party schools at different levels respectively are under the direct leadership of the party committee of their same level, and the official education management department performs its corresponding function. In terms of operation, the Party School of the CPC Central Committee provides the guidance for the party school of the CPC committee of each province (region, city), and takes a variety of measures to help local party schools improve their operations and the quality of their teaching. The party school implements the leadership system of the school council. The school council is responsible for the school's overall operation and its members are appointed by the party committee of the same level. The routine work of the school council is under the direction of the president or vice president of the institution. The party school presidents come from and work concurrently as party secretary or deputy party secretary of the same level. The vice president in charge of the routine work can be appointed as the chief official of the party committee department at the same level, and as a nominee for the party committee member of that level.

A party committee exercises its leadership over its corresponding party school in the following ways: (1) it passes on important decisions made by the CPC Central Committee and party committee at a higher level, brings the work of the party school into the overall work plan of the party committee and general arrangements to do with the structure of the party, works out solutions to problems concerning the reform and development of the party at regular intervals, and performs the function of supervision and inspection; (2) it formulates policies for official refresher training, and integrates the training of officials with their employment; (3) it appoints and assesses the leading group of the party school; (4) it sets up and develops the system in which responsible members of the party and government give lectures, deliver reports and have discussions with the participants in the party schools; (5) it helps the party school play the think-tank role to aid the decision-making of the party committee and the government; (6) it coordinates the departments concerned to support the work of the party school by providing sufficient conditions for the operations of the party school; (7) it holds the party school conference regularly to exchange experiences and deploy new commissions.

A party school and its party committee of a higher level instruct the operations of those at lower levels in the following aspects: (1) it investigates how the party schools of a lower-level party committee implement the guidelines and policies concerning the work of the party school that is issued by the Central Committee, and brings forward opinions and suggestions; (2) it investigates the teaching, research, faculty training, and information structure of the party schools of the lower level party committee, and puts forward ideas and suggestions for improving its work; (3) it formulates scientific measures and a system for evaluating the quality of education, and co-evaluates the work of the party schools of the lower-level party committee, along with the departments concerned; (4) the Party School of the Central Committee and the party school of each province, autonomous region, and municipality coordinate and supervise the compilation of textbooks, scientific research projects, disciplinary procedures, and degree evaluation of the party schools of the lower-level party committees; (5) it convenes the party school administrators' meeting of the lower-level party committees regularly to communicate information, summarize their experiences and carry out work investigations.

The system of schools of administration is under the direct leadership of the government departments. The *Regulations on Schools of Administration* explicitly stipulates that a school of administration is under the direct jurisdiction of the government. Schools of administration at different levels are under the leadership of the government departments of the same level. Specifically, the official education management department performs the management function. With regard to operations, the Chinese Academy of Governance is responsible for the operations guidance nationwide over schools of administration set up by each government at local level. The schools of administration established by the higher-level people's governments provide operations guidance for those at lower levels. The operations guidance includes: (1) putting forward suggestions on implementing the party's policies and guidelines concerning the work of schools of administration; (2) putting forward suggestions for improvement concerning teaching and training, scientific research, decision-making and consultation, faculty training, open teaching, and information collection; (3) formulating scientific evaluation measures and systems, and co-evaluating the operating performance of schools of administration established by the lower-level people's governments along with the civil service departments; (4) coordinating and supervising the compilation of textbooks, disciplinary procedures, scientific research projects, and cooperation and exchange; (5) strengthening the sharing of experience and information between schools of administration.

Each department and professional field has also built a party school or training centers with its own system for educating its cadres. These training institutions are under the leadership of the party committee of its department or professional field, whose training management department is generally set up within the organization department or personnel department of the party committee.

As for non-governmental or overseas training, we have established the access mechanism for institutions that are qualified for China's official education and training. After the evaluation of the training institutions, those that meet the requirements are granted permits for official training. After their training, we will organize the trainees to assess the training and teaching quality of these institutions, and take the results as important factors in deciding if these training institutions will be authorized to undertake training tasks in the future.

2. Functional division of all types of official education and training institutions

Among all types of official education and training institutions, the party schools, schools of administration, and leadership academies are the main channels and platforms for official education and training for the dissemination of theory, education in party spirit, and deployment of major policies and decisions of the country and the party.

Party schools are significant in providing refresher training and other such training for party leaders. They study and disseminate Marxism-Leninism, Mao Zedong Thought, Deng Xiaoping Theory, the important thoughts of the Three Represents, the Scientific Outlook on Development and the guiding principles of Comrade Xi Jinping's major speeches. The party schools function to enhance the party spirit. Under the direct leadership of the party committee, party schools cultivate party officials and theoretical leaders. The fundamental tasks of party schools are (1) training the party's officials at different levels; (2) training middle-aged and young party cadres; (3) training leading officials and enhancing the theoretical and ideological backbone of the departments; (4) coordinating with the departments of organization and personnel to assess and inspect the trainees during training; (5) developing scientific research by focusing on new conditions and problems both at home and abroad; (6) disseminating Marxism-Leninism, Mao Zedong Thought, Deng Xiaoping Theory the important thoughts of Three Represents, fully implementing the Scientific Outlook on Development, developing studies on and carrying out the guiding principles from Comrade Xi Jinping's major speeches, and publicizing the guidelines, principles and policies of the party.

Schools of administration are the main channels to train civil servants, foster public administration personnel and policy researchers, develop the theoretical research in sectors such as social science and public administration, and provide consultation on governing policies. The main functions of schools of administration are the following: (1) training civil servants; (2) training state-owned enterprise (SOE) leaders; (3) developing scientific research around the core work of the party and government as well as teaching requirements, and then putting forward policy proposals or recommendations to the party committee and government at different levels. Currently, the overwhelming majority of schools of administration and party schools at the provincial level are actually 'two names, one agency', serving the same cause, with some of the personnel focusing on the particular divisions of their work.

Each department and professional field respectively builds its own system of official education and training institutions in accordance with their responsibility to implement the education of their respective department and field. Official education and training institutions of the department and professional type are responsible for and play a key role in the official education and training in their specific area. They mainly train officials of all types and of different levels in the department and professional field, and carry out training tasks based on related requirements and the realities of their jobs. An official education and training institution of this type fulfills these tasks as follows: (1) it takes part in the formulation of the overall plan and annual plan for the official education and training of its department or professional field; (2) it carries out the training and subject research, on the core work of its relevant area; (3) it provides officials at different levels of its department or professional field with initial training, training for their post, professional training, and further education for professionals and technicians to improve their comprehensive quality and competence; (4) it develops curricula and teaching materials with its own characteristics; (5) it applies teaching and training methods corresponding to its characteristics; (6) it cooperates and communicates with other official education and training institutions.

The Organization Department of the CPC Central Committee Confirms First Batch of National Official Training Bases in Institutions of Higher Learning

On October 9, 2009, the Organization Department of the CPC Central Committee and Ministry of Education jointly issued *Opinions on Establishing and Regulating Official Training Bases in Institutions of Higher Learning*, confirming a batch of universities as the first national official training bases in institutions of higher learning. They are Peking University, Tsinghua University, Renmin University of China, Beijing Normal University, Fudan University, Xi'an Jiaotong University, Harbin Institute of Technology, Zhejiang University, Nanjing University, Sichuan University, Nankai University, Wuhan University and Sun Yat-sen University.

Institutions of higher learning and research are also a vital force for official education and training. They are specialized in higher education and scientific research, and enjoy strengths in the areas of discipline construction, specialized courses, and fundamental research. They have valuable experience in knowledge dissemination and skill training. We make full use of their advantages in resources, and authorize them to implement the official education and training tasks in the aspects of new knowledge and new skills. With further development of official education and training, some institutions of higher learning and research give full play to their advantages, are actively involved in official education and training work, and have achieved substantial results. It has been found that institutions of higher learning and research significantly supplement official education and training. Their training of new knowledge and new skills cultivates competition, and helps to relieve the stress of insufficient resources in official education and training, making their respective advantages complementary to each other, and improving the efficiency of educational and scientific resources. Institutions of higher learning and research lay emphasis on intensifying cooperation with the official education and training management department and the institutions that officials work at to co-found the official training bases and jointly run schools serving large-scale official training. In 2010, the Organization Department of the CPC Central Committee and the Ministry of Education confirmed 13 institutions of higher learning, such as Peking University and Tsinghua University, as national official education and training bases.

In addition, the official education and training management department authorizes the official training programs of eligible non-government and overseas training institutions, which themselves accept the commission to undertake the programs. A non-government training institution refers to a training institution that is approved by relevant administrative departments of the state. As an independent legal entity, it is responsible for its own management decisions, profits and losses. Non-government training institutions include organizations affiliated to institutions of higher learning which provide specialized knowledge training, schools run with social organizations, and institutions run jointly with other countries. These training institutions boast comparative advantages in specialized knowledge and skill training in terms of their initiative as well as their flexibility and specialization. Based on the actual demands of official education and training, the management department commissions the eligible non-government training institutions to carry out official education and training programs. In order to meet the requirements of opening up to the outside world and all-round diplomacy and serve the general prospect of diplomacy, we pick those that are qualified among national and local training institutions to conduct official education and training. We pay special attention to choosing prestigious overseas universities, research institutions and transnational corporations to implement official education and training. The management department reinforces the supervision of the overseas training process in the aspects of organizational leadership, operation mechanism and program requirements. First, it develops domestic pre-training, informing the participants of the training content, arrangements and requirements in advance. Second, it strengthens overseas team management. It guides participants in experiencing the benefits of learning abroad, enhancing their political sensitivity while remaining politically sober and firm and advocating the self-managing and self-serving functions of the team. Third, it tracks the results of overseas training and promotes the sharing and improvement of results.

At present, there are over 5,200 training institutions of all types above county level in China, and up to 100,000 staff engaged in the education and training of officials. Over four million trainees may be trained in schools at any one time. With its impressive scale and adequate level of teaching and research, the Chinese system of educating and training officials meets the needs of the party and the nation.

3. Functions and tasks of official education and training institutions at different levels

The party schools, schools of administration and leadership academies are the major channels and platforms of China's official education and training. Official education and training institutions at the national level are responsible for the training of senior officials nationwide, and the local and grassroots party schools of the province, city and county are responsible for the training of officials at the local level.

Official education and training institutions at the national level, such as the Party School of the CPC Central Committee, the Chinese Academy of Governance, CELAP, CELAJ and CELAY mainly train leaders nationwide at the levels of province, ministry, and bureau. They have their respective functions, and focus on official training from different perspectives. The Party School of the CPC Central Committee provides officials with education on Marxist theory, helps them consolidate their theoretical basis, broadens their global vision, cultivates their strategic thinking, and enhances their party spirit. The Chinese Academy of Governance offers training on improving administrative ability, governing by law and public administration for civil servants, while also training senior management personnel and policy researchers. CELAP, CELAJ and CELAY are the bases for the education of revolutionary traditions and of basic national conditions. They are also vital to the improvement of the quality and competence of leading officials, and act as a window for international training exchange and cooperation. CELAP mainly focuses its training on reform and opening up, socialism with Chinese characteristics, and knowledge and skills concerning modernization. CELAJ and CELAY offer education on party history, party spirit and party conduct, as well as on the party's theory of construction, revolutionary traditions and basic national conditions to the leaders as training participants.

The party school and school of administration at the provincial level are responsible for the training of officials from their own province. A party school fulfills six basic tasks. They (1) offer training and refresher training to the party's leading officials and reserve officials at different levels and cultivate theoretical leaders; (2) organize seminars held by the party committee and government; (3) carry out scientific research on new situations and problems both at home and abroad, undertake research tasks assigned by the party committee and government, and promote theoretical innovation; (4) target significant theoretical and practical problems in the process of reform and opening up in socialist modernization, carry out theoretical dissemination of the latest achievements in the implementation of Marxism in China, and publicize the party's line, principles and policies; (5) implement the further education and training of officials such as in the form of degree programs, in light of the laws, regulations and policies of the country; (6) cooperate and communicate with overseas education and research institutions and organizations.

Schools of administration perform their major responsibilities in the following aspects. They (1) train civil servants, management personnel of SOEs, policy researchers, hold seminars conducted by the party committee and government, and carry out commissioned programs and joint training; (2) develop research on philosophy and social science, and research on theoretical and practical problems in the fields of administrative restructuring, scientific administration, administration by law, social administration, and public service; (3) develop decision-making consultation mainly for the party committee and government; (4) The Chinese Academy of Governance and other eligible local schools of administration cooperate and exchange with organizations concerned both at home and abroad; (5) The Chinese Academy of Governance, in view of the laws, regulations and policies concerned, offers postgraduate programs; (6) undertake other affairs assigned by the government.

4. Characteristics of official education and training institutions of all types

Party schools highlight education in party theory. Under the direct leadership of the party committee, it is aimed at producing the party's leading officials and theoretical officials. It is a base for the study, research and dissemination of the significant strategic thinking, namely, Marxism-Leninism, Mao Zedong Thought, Deng Xiaoping Theory, the important thoughts of Three Represents, the Scientific Outlook on Development, and the guiding principles from Comrade Xi Jinping's major speeches. Party schools have formulated the teaching curriculum to cover the theoretical basis of the party, its global outlook, strategic thinking, and to cultivate the party spirit. They focus on the study of significant strategic thinking, such as Deng Xiaoping Theory, the important thoughts of the Three Represents, the Scientific Outlook on Development and the guiding principles from Comrade Xi Jinping's major speeches, so as to improve the leadership quality and governing capability of officials. They emphasize the latest achievements and innovations in theory to consolidate the theoretical basis of the party in trainees. They stress the current international economic and political situations to broaden the global vision of trainees. They strengthen trainees' awareness of the overall situation and address how to deal with complex situations to enhance the strategic thinking of trainees. They attach importance to the concept of striving for goals and improving work methods to improve the party spirit of trainees.

A school of administration gives priority to improving administrative ability. A school of administration determines the theme and arranges training content by focusing on the central task and serving the overall interests of the party. It sets up the school system and training classes, and fulfills training tasks by closely integrating the construction of teams of civil servants with the governmental reality. The Chinese Academy of Governance is oriented to 'public administration', and actively constructs and completes the new teaching and training module characterized as having 'one central core of improving civil servants' quality and competency, and three key points of public servant awareness, modern administration, and governing by law', known in short as 'one core, three key points'. Centered on teaching, but guided by consultation and based on research, schools of administration at different levels stick to the principle of 'three-in-one', that is, integrating teaching, research and consultation into an organic whole, evident in their civil servant training, public administration research and policy consultation.

Other leadership academies endeavor to identify their own functions, rely on their own special official education resources, and develop their potential and strengths. For example, CELAP, CELAJ and CELAY use their unique advantages to form distinctive methods and characteristics in the running of their schools. Based on the Central Committee's requirements, these three leadership academies constructed themselves into new training platforms for officials to learn and practice Deng Xiaoping Theory and the important thoughts of the Three Represents, firmly establish their Scientific Outlook on Development, and to put into practice the guiding principles from Comrade Xi Jinping's major speeches. They are suitable for diversified, professional, high-level, and large-scale official training, and also for the reform and innovation of official education and training. The major training responsibilities of these three leadership academies are as follows: (1) carrying out part of the training tasks of the party and government officials, including part of the classes and courses of the Party School of the CPC Central Committee, the Chinese Academy of Governance and other leadership academies; (2) undertaking part of the training tasks of enterprise executives and administrative personnel of public institutions; (3) undertaking part of the training tasks of senior professionals and technicians; (4) training some of the officials in military academies; (5) fulfilling other training tasks entrusted by the CPC Central Committee.

These distinctive characteristics and unique advantages of the three leadership academies allow them to take full advantage of the resources of the revolutionary tradition and modernization achievements for official training. They utilize their respective advantages to form unique methods for running their schools. Relying on and developing their unique official education resources, they strove to transform the former residences and sites during the revolutionary period into classrooms, the abundant historical materials into vivid teaching materials, and the sites of reform, opening up and modern construction into teaching bases. CELAP embodies the characteristics of internalization, contemporaneity and openness. In passing on modern economic management theory and knowledge, it enhances the ability of trainees to think strategically, helps them develop a global vision, broadens their knowledge, fortifies their aim of building socialism with Chinese characteristics, and improves their ability to lead modern construction. CELAJ and CELAY rely heavily on their advantages in revolutionary resources to carry on party traditions, teach party history and basic national conditions, improve the ideological and political quality of trainees and cultivate their party spirit to maintain their passion for revolutionary principles.

II. Training Base Construction

1. Aims and tasks of training base construction

The *Regulations on Official Education and Training Work (Trial)* states that the principal goals of constructing a system of official education and training institutions are the clear division of work, having respective advantages that are complementary to each other, a reasonable layout, and orderly competition. In this system, official education and training is conducted primarily by institutions such as party schools, schools of administration and leadership academies, with institutions of higher learning, research institutes and other training institutions extending and supplementing the training. The characteristics of the system of institutions must be as follows. The first is the clear division of work. Official education and training institutions of different types at different levels have explicit functions, and must solve problems where there is an unclear division of work, a lack of clear-cut job responsibility, a waste of resources and where the school does not run efficiently. The second is that their respective advantages must complement each other. The education and training institutions of different types at different levels utilize the management of their schools and their advantages, strengthen cooperation, and complement each other in forming the overall system of schools. The third is having a reasonable layout. When the major channels for official education and training are constructed, the integration of training institutions is boosted so that official education and training institutions of different types and at different levels are reasonably distributed in terms of locations and functions, and are realized on an economically efficient scale. The fourth is orderly competition. The education and training institutions of different types should rely on their respective advantages, learn from each other, compete fairly, develop jointly and improve simultaneously. The *Regulations* states that the official education and training management department should formulate and implement corresponding access standards, and establish assessment systems for official education and training institutions. The management department should adopt and develop rules for the official education and training market, guide official education and training institutions to optimize services, and improve their quality, so as to form an official education and training market mechanism characterized by openness, equality, and orderly competition, guided by the department in charge of official education and training. It should implement the management system of official education and training. The management department can take measures such as direct commission, bidding and tendering to grant permits for qualified training institutions to enter the market, as well as to tighten the management of program implementation and improve training performance.

The *Reform Program* proposes to construct a more open official education and training framework. The Organization Department of the CPC Central Committee and the provincial organization department (also in autonomous regions and municipalities) can utilize the high-quality resources of institutions of higher learning to carry out the training on new theory, new knowledge, new skills and new information. They can take advantage of the rich resources, initiate diversified bases for practice, teaching and research, and provide vibrant classrooms for trainees to strengthen their abilities and their party spirit. They encourage and guide eligible non-government training institutions to engage in official education and training. Maintaining the guideline of 'taking the initiative, adapting others' methods to our needs, drawing on advantages and avoiding mistakes, and emphasizing practical results', they actively take advantage of prestigious overseas universities and other training institutions to carry out official training. They develop international cooperation and exchange in the training of leadership talent. They accelerate the setting up of the network platform for official education and training. To meet the demands set by the rapid development of modern information technology, they strengthen the network training infrastructure, standardize official network training management, and better satisfy the diversified learning requirements of officials. They integrate the existing network training resources, and build an open, inclusive and shared national official education and training network. The standardized and efficient official network training system featuring complete functions and shared resources was fully established by 2012.

2. Training base construction measures

(1) Resource integration

We stress the integration and optimization of training institutions, and continuously improve the running of schools. The *Reform Program* stipulates that we should boost the reform of the system by which schools are run, and form a layout where party schools, schools of administration and leadership academies utilize their major roles, institutions of higher learning and other training providers are actively involved, and network training is widely applied. This layout with complementary advantages is competitive and vibrant. Whether the system of schools is scientific or not determines the vitality of the running of the schools, as well as the optimal allocation of resources and benefits of their utilization. In terms of reforming the school system, we should boost the integration and optimization of the major training channels and bases, focusing on enhancing the reform of the party schools at city and county levels. The county-level party school can be taken as the branch school of the city-level party school, or can be integrated with other training resources of the same administrative region, so as to extend the training functions of the county-level party schools. District-level party schools that are not eligible under the jurisdiction of the city and the county-level party schools should be reduced and reconstructed. The aim of the reform of the party school system is, by means of resource integration and optimization, to feasibly strengthen the running of the schools. The second task of system reform is to integrate and optimize official education and training institutions of a department or professional field. Ministries and commissions under the CPC Central Committee and state organs should take overall consideration of the quantity of training tasks, degree of professionalization, market substitutability and optimization and integration of the training institutions under their control. Each province, region and city should integrate subordinate training institutions with similar functions and operations, but should not rebuild them to avoid redundancy. The department and professional field training institutions at the levels of city and county should be gradually closed except for special reasons. By means of reform, we will further highlight the unique features of the department and professional training institutions and improve their competence.

(2) An open school system

We insist on running schools openly and getting the most out of a variety of quality training resources to serve official education and training. First we must construct a more extensive training layout. We will break the comparatively closed and self-sustaining system of official education and training institutions, and bring institutions of higher learning, qualified non-government training institutions and overseas quality resources into the official education and training system, and thereby constantly extend the scope of the training system. The second point is to gradually integrate the existing network of training resources, continuously expand the coverage of the training, and build an open, inclusive, and shared official education and training network system. It is important to select quality teachers from various areas for official education and training, and to increase the employment of part-time teachers. We make the best of practical resources to serve official education and training, and have signed agreements with many local government sectors, institutions of higher learning, research institutes and large-scale enterprises. A large number of training programs design extensive practical and experiential courses where officials are required to conduct on-the-spot investigation and study. We also cooperate and exchange with some government sectors, institutions of higher learning and research institutes to carry out research, to arrange teachers to take posts in training bases, with the aim of promoting official education and training to potential trainees, elevating the level of the school and improving teaching quality. Of the 2,000-plus institutions of higher learning nationwide, many have become important forces for official education and training. Peking University and Tsinghua University train 10,000 or so officials annually. No other political party in the world is on par with the CPC, which boasts such a large-scale school running system as the solid foundation for the development of official education and training, and for the party itself. Official education and training institutions offer initiative services to local government sectors, institutions of higher learning and enterprises, and also undertake program research, carry out joint research and train officials for these sectors and organizations. In addition, we utilize the advantages of overseas official education and training to serve domestic official education and training. We emphasize the benefits of cooperating and exchanging with overseas education and

A revolutionary veteran teaching revolutionary history to students of Yan'an Cadre Academy (Xinhua News Agency)

training institutions. Official education and training institutions of all types, through their joint training courses, mutually designate exchange students and visiting scholars, employ guest professors, jointly undertake research projects and hold seminars. This intensifies the exchange and cooperation with institutions of higher learning, research institutes, non-government training institutions, overseas training institutions and related international organizations in areas featuring disciplinary systems, teachers, teaching and research facilities, teaching materials, libraries and information. We also effectively utilize various overseas training resources to serve China's official education and training. In recent years, overseas training has developed, and over 4,000 participants have been trained overseas. The Organization Department of the CPC Central Committee has developed long-term cooperation programs with transnational corporations, such as the United Nations Development Program (UNDP), GE in the USA, Nokia in Finland, and with world-renowned universities including Oxford, Cambridge and Harvard, and with government departments in Japan, Korea, Singapore, and Hong Kong. Each province, region and city has also developed some overseas training channels.

(3) Competition and selection

In some areas measures are taken to boost competition among training institutions over time, in order to stimulate dynamism in the school system. For example, by means of bids and tenders, some regions encourage competition for planned programs among the party schools, schools of administration, leadership academies, institutions of higher learning and other non-government institutions, and choose institutions to carry this out. The *Reform Program* points out that it is vital to increase competition among training institutions. Between the party schools, schools of administration, leadership academies, and between official education and training institutions, institutions of higher learning and other non-governmental institutions, the mechanism of competition and selection should be established to guide training institutions to develop their overall quality. The first step is to establish the access system of official education and training institutions, strictly examine qualifications, further foster new types of training bodies, making education and training more open, competitive and selective in practice, while avoiding repeated bullish investments with low returns. The second is to build the program management system of official education and training, adopt the method of bids and tenders, direct consignment and outsourcing, and to select institutions through competition to guide quality resources towards the field of official education and training. The third is to strengthen the supervision and management of the official education and training market and to ensure fair participation, standardized operation, and freedom of access and withdrawal. We are exploring ways to gradually implement the bidding and tendering system for training programs, to establish the access system of official education and training institutions, and conduct competition and selection among official education and training institutions nationwide. Furthermore, we carry out autonomous learning in official education and training institutions at the national level. At the end of each year when the training plan of the next year is being formed, each official education and training institution at the national level firstly designs the planned training themes and classes, and then sends them down to local organization departments, providing resources for officials to choose and apply them autonomously. Finally the Official Education Bureau of the Organization Department of the CPC Central Committee confirms the next year's training plan of each national-level official training institution based on the choices of the trainees. If a training class does not have many applicants, the class will be cancelled. This effectively motivates competition among national-level training institutions, and drives each training institution to utilize their respective advantages and to make great efforts to improve the quality of training and teaching.

3. Training base operation

Official education and training institutions of all types strictly implement the requirements of the CPC Central Committee, form an in-depth understanding of the demands of economic and social development, actively explore new thinking and approaches to reform and development, pay attention to the demands of officials during training, and earnestly examine critical current issues and the difficulties that officials are concerned with in their practical work. They draw fully on experiences from the new concepts, new knowledge, new measures and new techniques of modern education and training. They summarize the latest experiences and results of education and training activities, and constantly apply new ideas to training content and methods.

The first is the setting of class schedules. In light of the overall situation of the party and the state, official education and training institutions of different types and levels take into consideration their respective functions and training requirements of a specific region or department, determined by the state of economic and social development and their priorities for further development. Based on the factors above and the level and type of the training tasks the institutions carry out, they analyze the demands and needs of officials of the organization departments, and then determine the training themes and design classes.

In the process of setting up the class schedule, we follow the principle of 'classification and stratification'. Classification is the process by which training classes are arranged in accordance with the distinctive features and development of each official, in order to effectively enhance the relevance and attractiveness of training to officials. The classes are scheduled with new content, prominent features, are varied, and cater to a variety of diverse official teams in terms of their professional system, field and specific posts. For instance, the training classes and refresher training programs (further education) of the party school system are oriented to different types of officials and have different characteristics, functions and tasks. One type is promotion-oriented training, which aims to provide relevant officials with systematic training on theory, knowledge, ability and integrity before they assume their new positions, and to equip them with corresponding qualifications. Refresher training programs feature on-the-job updated training which arranges for officials involved to leave their work temporarily and enjoy a period of full-time training in corresponding training institutions after they have held the post for some time, so that they can obtain information on the latest important theories and solutions to practical problems, in order to further enhance their theoretical level and problem-solving ability.

Stratification is where official education and training institutions at different levels, in accordance with the system division and their respective work orientation, set up corresponding training classes to meet the levels of the officials. For example, currently, the Party School of the CPC Central Committee mainly offers refresher training to party officials at the province and ministry levels, senior party officials in government departments and bureaus, and party secretaries at the county level. Provincial party schools (in autonomous regions and municipalities) are responsible for the refresher training of deputy leaders of department or bureau level and party officials at county or division level. Regional party schools (city) are oriented to train deputy party officials at county or division level, and some officials at the township level. Party schools at county (city) level focus on refresher training for some party officials at township and prefecture level, and secretaries in grassroots party branches. Party schools at different levels set up refresher training classes for officials of different levels according to their work division. We arrange the schedule of all types of training classes in accordance with the training themes, the features of training classes, and practical demands of participants. Judging from practical experience, medium- and long-term training are the major channels for officials, and in particular for young officials to build a solid theoretical foundation with a grasp of theories and knowledge via systematic learning. Short-term training is effective in improving the ability of officials, particularly in terms of solving practical problems, understanding and mastering certain theories and knowledge in a short period of time. Besides the medium and long-term training focusing on theories, official education and training institutions offer short-term training classes with clear objectives, distinct topics, rich content, and diversified forms on the basis of the rules of the development of the officials and their actual conditions. Their advantages are that they are short, effective, practical and flexible, and enlarge the scale of official training. For example, of the training classes held by the Party School of the CPC Central Committee, some classes last one year, others half a year and some only a couple of months. The schooling of the Central Party School lasts comparatively longer than that of other schools. The Chinese Academy of Governance, CELAP, local party schools and schools of administration usually hold classes for several months for long-term training, and for short-term training classes they are held for less than a month or less than 10 days.

The second is the operation procedure. In each training institution, generally speaking, the department or office of teaching affairs (the latter are set up by local party schools) is responsible for the management of the school's teaching. The teaching management department formulates the annual training plan, and implements it after it is approved by the management department of official education and training. The teaching management department is also responsible for formulating the teaching plan, organizing teaching, implementing management and evaluating teaching performance. When the annual training plan is settled, the teaching management department together with the organization department assigns participants to classes with the fixed school schedule. Once a concrete teaching plan for a certain class is approved by the leader who supervises the teaching, the teaching faculty designs and develops corresponding courses. The training institution is in charge of the management of trainees, which involves class organization and training project implementation. After the completion of each training program or training class, the management department records the experience, evaluates its implementation, and provides feedback in preparation for the next training class.

III. Construction of Educational Discipline

Discipline is a fundamental element attributed to the quality and efficiency of official education and training, and a good training discipline guarantees effective training. Integrating theory with practice is the party's tradition, and this principle also functions as an essential training discipline. President Xi Jinping attaches great importance to building the discipline of officials, requiring them to place study at the top of their training agenda. Throughout the entire process of official education and training, we consistently adhere to the Marxist discipline of integrating theory with practice. We do this by rigorously following the principles of strict administration, management, and education in the training of officials. We lay emphasis on incorporating the study of theory with problem-solving regarding China's practical difficulties, learning to meet practical needs, and improving the capacity to analyze and resolve problems with a Marxist viewpoint and methods.

1. Adhering to the principle of integrating theory with practice throughout the process of official education and training

The primary purpose of the further education of officials is to improve their work competence and their ability to solve practical problems.

During the teaching and training of officials in institutions, we adhere to taking Marxist theory as the main course, organize officials to deeply study the basic tenets of Marxism, and focus on the theoretical system of socialism with Chinese characteristics, so that their minds are armed with the party's latest theoretical achievements to guide and push forward their work. We ensure the cultivation of party spirit and style by organizing officials to study the party constitution, the history of the party and the country, the party's traditional style and its core socialist values, and by guiding them to behave morally and with strong ethics. We also embed the party's line, principles and policies as well as national laws and regulations into elementary courses, and ensure that the education and training of officials is up-to-date with the party's decisions.

In terms of the teaching, research and management carried out by official education and training institutions, we adhere to the principle of integrating theory with practice consistently. In teaching, we pay attention to investigating social practical problems and the needs of officials, and we design classes, offer courses, and define teaching themes and content in accordance with the concept of being oriented towards needs and centered on problems. In terms of research, we closely connect principal theories concerning economic and social development and the party's construction with practical problems. We conduct research by linking officials' posts and practical work with their thinking, and gain valuable results and outcomes from consulting them. Regarding management, we set up scientific and reasonable rules and regulations, formulate a set of assessment methods to facilitate the creation of training discipline, and strive to promote good training discipline within a perfected system.

In the training arrangement for teachers, we require them to take reality into account, and then organize teaching activities focused on the study of significant practical problems concerning some major issues in the reform and opening up, and modernization of China. We also ask teachers to hold the correct political direction and principles in their handling of issues and difficulties put forward by trainees in their learning process, in order to enhance the persuasive power of theoretical education. Teachers should organize trainees and lead them in profound theoretical reflection, to deepen their learning by focusing on working out solutions to problems encountered at work, to improve their ideological and theoretical levels and to improve their ability to analyze and pragmatically resolve problems.

We also require that trainees learn by adhering to the principle of integrating theory with practice in official education and training institutions. Trainees should integrate theoretical learning and research with practical problem solving, and integrate their study of the party's innovative theory with the practice of building a moderately prosperous society in all respects and deepening reform and opening up. They should transform each strategic deployment and requirement to correct ideas and policy measures for the local development of their relevant department or professional field, and solve important problems in reform and development. At the same time, we require that trainees integrate their study of the party's innovative theory with the practice of enhancing their party spirit, effectively resolve issues concerning their individual thinking, and strengthen the transformation of the subjective world. In learning to pursue the communist spirit and moral sentiments, official trainees may conquer some obvious shortcomings existing in their thinking, work style and conduct.

We also lay emphasis on guiding teachers and trainees to integrate theory with practice in teaching and learning by means of assessment and evaluation. We take the ability of teachers in applying theory to practice as the main index of assessing their teaching level and evaluating the learning performance of trainees. Teaching is judged by whether theoretical teaching is integrated with reform, opening up and socialist modernization, and whether teachers can answer questions with theories by linking trainees' work practice with the theoretical problems they face. The performance of trainees is judged by whether they can apply the theory and knowledge they have learned to form opinions and suggestions to address practical problems, as well as by the development in their ideological style and work achievements.

2. Adhering to principles of strict administration, strict management and strict education

Official education and training is a key element of party building. In the education and training of officials, we adhere to the notion that 'the party manages, governs and conducts in a strict way', particularly in its strict requirements and administration process.

The first is strict administration. We require that official education and training institutions reinforce their ideological and political structure and their work style, strengthen management to run schools diligently and economically, and with regulations to enforce discipline.

The second is strict management. We put the strict requirements of cultivating academic morals and rigorous scholarship on teaching faculties to ensure that they are examples for officials and models for society. In teaching activities, we stick to research without restraints and teaching with discipline, and maintaining the seriousness of teaching. Teachers are not allowed to propagate ideas that go against the party's theories, line, discipline, and policies, or that are against the decisions of the CPC Central Committee. We take various measures, such as learning, training and practice to improve teachers' ideological and political quality and their ability to integrate theory with practice, in which strict management is implemented.

The third is strict education. We see it as not only the right thing to do for officials to participate in learning and training, but also a duty and obligation. We require officials to take part in organizational training, and to treat the training seriously, as they are responsible for the party's and people's cause. They are not allowed to learn only based on personal habits, interests and hobbies. We deliberately formulate regulations to strengthen the structure of training discipline and trainee management. We require training institutions to strictly follow relevant regulations and manage trainees effectively. Training institutions should come up with detailed rules for the implementation of trainee management, which require them to participate in learning as ordinary students in training institutions and to abide by school regulations.

Chapter 5

Who Teaches

Strengthening the construction of teaching faculties is an essential function of official education and training, and it is of key importance to maintain an adequate amount of teachers with high capacity and a complete coverage of academic disciplines to improve the overall quality of training. To meet the demand for excellent teachers, we have made many efforts to develop official education and training faculties, aiming for high quality, proper size, sound organization, and full-time and part-time teachers who complement each other. First, high quality. We select and recruit high-quality talent into teaching faculties. We generally require them to be reliable in terms of ideological and political quality, professional ethics, to have high-level theoretical ability for interpreting policy, solid expertise, sufficient working experience, mastery of modern educational theory and skills, and competence in teaching and research. Second, proper size. Aiming for excellence and efficiency, we scientifically establish a reasonable size for the teaching faculty based on a comprehensive analysis of the needs of the institution, its functions and orientation, training participants, training scope and other factors relevant to official education and training. Third, sound organization. We constantly optimize the structure of teaching faculties depending on the level and kind of training to ensure that the composition of the team stays in proportion in terms of expertise, age, academic qualifications, rank and position, and to ensure that there are both full-time and part-time teachers. Fourth, complementing full-time and part-time teachers. While building a team of full-time quality teachers, we also make full use of social resources to invite distinguished talent as our guest lecturers to complete the educational and training tasks for officials. We have established an official education and training team with both full-time and part-time teachers, who make the aims of the education and training of officials possible and successful, and commit to the constant improvement of the quality of the education and training.

I. Full-time Teaching Faculties
1. Current state of full-time teaching faculties

At present, there are more than 100,000 full-time teachers nationwide in official education and training institutions of all levels, of which there are over 20,000 teachers with professional senior titles.

Every training institution selects and employs teaching faculty members with excellent talent, according to the relevant requirements of their post. When they select teachers who will be suitable for their own school, they generally consider these factors: the knowledge system, age proportion, degree proportion, expertise proportion and work experience, along with the realities of the school, the need for official qualifications compatible with local economic and social development, and the general condition of the institution concerned.

In the Central Party School, the Chinese Academy of Governance (previously named China National School of Administration) and every provincial party school (including those of autonomous regions and municipalities) and schools of administration, full-time teachers mainly teach classes and conduct professional research. Besides these jobs, full-time teachers in some schools also design curricula, organize seminars and research specific subjects for the classes they are in charge of. For

A teacher at CELAP commenting on students' plans for handling public hazards (Ren Long, Xinhua News Agency)

example, at CELAP, the permanent teaching faculty members play an important role in professionally designing the development of teaching, researching and curricula of official education and training. Informed by the principle of 'fewer in quantity but better in quality', CELAP has built up a high-level professional faculty of highly qualified teachers with a logical structure. There are about 60 full-time teachers, which is over a quarter of overall staff members. They all have doctorates and senior professional titles, and 20% of them have overseas study experience. Some 80% of the group are aged under 40. Since the inception of the academy, these permanent teachers have been shouldering a major task of course development. They have opened more than 1,000 courses, including more than 600 training programs based on over 260 spots for field studies. Some courses developed by young teachers have received widespread recognition from their trainees. The establishment of full-time teaching faculties guarantees the fundamental and normal operation of CELAP's teaching.

2. Building full-time teaching teams

We have a standardized procedure for recruitment, management and assessment to attract extraordinary talent to our education and training faculty. To ensure that they are of high quality, we assign them to do a lot of practical work and also arrange training for them to enhance their professional competence. While selecting and recruiting full-time teachers, we try deliberately to expand the range of their backgrounds. Some of them are well known scholars from higher learning institutions and research institutes. Some are outstanding graduates from universities. Others are excellent party or administrative officials or entrepreneurs who are willing to commit to official education and training, and complement our existing teaching faculty. To improve the quality and ability of current faculty members, we request that they: go to other institutions to further their study, take field trips to conduct investigation and research, and serve in temporary positions to gain practical work experience.

To strengthen the construction of full-time teaching faculties, efforts made to develop and improve the management system are as follows:

First is the implementation of the appointment system. Based on teachers' existing professional titles, official education and training institutions assign them to different professional and technical posts at certain intervals, according to their teaching performance and academic achievements. The distinction of appointments between professional and technical titles enables different teachers to enjoy their corresponding rewards. Thus, this system has resolved the problems that teachers face in politics and in their lives, and can incentivize teachers to continuously improve their quality and ability.

Second is the implementation of the competition system. Competition is where teachers are selected for suitable positions in open competition while teaching and researching, which provides a solid basis for the appointment system. There are three types of competition: competition for the instructor's qualification for the main classes, open competition for lecturing posts in specific subjects, and competition for leadership posts in teaching and research.

Third is to establish and improve the appraisal system with awards and penalties. Assessing regular teaching is an important way of helping teachers to acknowledge their instructional position, and also a principal measure to maintain their passion and initiative to enhance their work, in that rewards and punishments are issued relevant to evaluation results. We attach importance to the assessment of teaching and research as well as other aspects, and then link the results with income distribution. We also take the appraisal results as an important reference for the assignment of professional titles and appointment of leadership posts. Because official education and training has not only the features of higher and adult education but also characteristics of its own, it is inappropriate for the institutions to wholly adopt appraisal methods and standards from the university evaluation system. The *Regulations on Official Education and Training Work (Trial)* therefore states that we must 'gradually establish the faculty appraisal system relevant to the characteristics of official education and training'. Furthermore, the *Reform Program* requests that we 'deepen the reform of the personnel system of official education and training institutions', 'research and set up a logical appraisal system appropriate to the characteristics of official education and training, and work out an effective method for professional title evaluation and post appointment'.

Fourth is to establish a cultivation system to develop the teaching faculty of official education and training. The *Regulations on Official Education and Training Work (Trial)* calls for forming mechanisms to update the knowledge of full-time teachers, and requires that 'the total duration for the annual experiential training of full-time faculty members is no less than one month'. The *Reform Program* emphasizes the cultivation of the teaching team and the implementation of training projects for trainers, and also proposes to 'plan step by step to organize and send excellent teachers, especially those who are young and middle-aged and the backbone of their working units and key part of their faculty, to further their study in prestigious universities at home and abroad, or to receive training in their higher-level official education and training institutions', and to 'effectively improve the capability of teachers to connect theory with practice and enhance their professional level by putting them in temporary work positions, field trips to research, and required classes to follow'. The *Plan for National Official Education and Training from 2013 to 2017* clearly states that we must 'strengthen the faculty development of national institutions in official education and training, cultivate and establish a team of distinguished educators and young or middle-aged prestigious scholars', 'carry out the plan for training excellent teachers: national institutions annually train 1,500 key teachers from local official education and training institutions; within five years, provincial party schools (schools of administration) train in turn all teachers from city and county-level training schools'.

In practice, regional institutions of all levels should establish their own mechanism to update the knowledge of their full-time teachers and to strengthen the development of their teaching faculties. Several systems have been developed, which are the following five general types. First, on-the-job education: to enrich their knowledge, teachers from local official education and training institutions are selected and sent to other countries, to higher-level training institutions, or to tertiary education institutions to further their study, and are granted funds to take degree courses and gain academic degrees via network education, long-distance education and other educational facilities. Second, temporary post service: young teachers who function as the backbone of their work units are organized to serve in an executive position in a local government or other administrative agency to strengthen their competence in tackling practical work. Third, social practice: to deepen their understanding of the state of our country, teachers are arranged systematically to conduct social investigation, subject-specific research and to participate in other activities either in foreign countries, or domestically in old revolutionary sites, impoverished or developed areas. Fourth, academic exchanges: teachers are encouraged to take part in academic exchanges and seminars to explore pedagogy or teaching methodology relevant to the education and training of officials with the goal of improving their teaching capability. Fifth, on-the-job learning: teachers are required to sit in some classes in their own school to observe teaching methods or to learn from important academic lectures. The development and improvement of these systems are conducive to improving the education and training of teachers and thereby raising their quality and capabilities to a higher level.

> **Case 8 CELAP's Research and Practice in Building Full-time Teaching Faculties**
>
> When building a team of full-time teachers, the steps taken are as follows:
>
> 1. Persistent public recruitment with a high starting point, and making efforts to construct a teaching team that is high in quality and properly sized. Adhering to the principle of 'high threshold and strict requirements', the academy is open to all scholars nationwide for recruitment. During this process, we have developed a rational recruiting procedure according to our requirements based on scientific tests. Steps taken in the procedure go as follows: (1) A political investigation is conducted to make sure that prospective teachers fit the political requirement; (2) A professional interview by a panel of experts and a comprehensive appraisal by CELAP leaders are designed to ensure that teachers are suitable for official training in terms of professional expertise and overall teaching quality; (3) To fit CELAP's international agenda, a foreign language application test is arranged for the applicants; (4) A psychological test is also arranged to assess the applicants' adaptability to teamwork. Through strict screening, CELAP selects from among over 10,000 applicants, and employs those who are qualified for the current full-time teaching faculty.
>
> 2. Building a teaching team in a 'matrix structure' combined with a 'subject group' and a project team to stress the teachers' leading role in official education and training. CELAP has set up five teaching and research departments and centers for case development and teaching practice, namely: the departments of economics and business administration; politics and public management; law and humanities; leadership education; and international exchange. With the set of 'five departments under one center', we organize teachers in terms of subject for the improvement of their academic achievements. Meanwhile, CELAP has flexibly set up some open-ended project groups such as the 'Mayor Development Research Group' around its training tasks, and the academy has also established cross-subject research institutions such as the Yangtze River Delta Research Institute, the Research Institute for Socialism with Chinese Characteristics, and the Leadership Research Institute. We gather teachers of

different subjects with different academic backgrounds together for mutual encouragement and improvement through the cooperation of project groups and research institutes. This teaching team within the matrix structure not only meets the training requirements and promotes the development of academic disciplines, but also improves the growth of our team.

3. Making efforts to improve the professional work of teachers by multi-channel training. To meet teaching requirements and raise the level of teaching, we have taken a series of effective steps. (1) Strengthening post training to encourage teachers to step onto the platform as soon as possible. CELAP organizes teachers to prepare lessons collectively, to give simulation lessons, and to take part in activities such as the 'demonstration of young teachers' style' to improve their teaching level. After we contact the community-level party schools and schools of administration, teachers can undergo training at these schools. We help them embark as soon as possible by arranging for them to practice firstly in classes without a plan and then to teach in classes within a plan. (2) Reinforcing teachers' social practice to help them familiarize themselves with the needs and characteristics of the trainees. We select teachers with doctorates to join a volunteer service group, appoint them to temporary posts in the party and government offices, and organize them to conduct investigations before training and to pay return visits after training nationwide, where they can get in touch with students and the wider society and reinforce their abilities to connect theory with practice. (3) Organizing research projects to strengthen the ability of teachers to investigate and resolve practical problems. We encourage our teachers to actively apply for research projects at national or ministerial and provincial level, about the cause of the party and country and also about official education and training courses. Our school also has set up a quantity of college-level research projects. Meanwhile, we appoint teachers to attend international academic seminars and take advanced studies abroad to improve their global communications capability. (4) Employing young teachers boldly and advocating the philosophy that 'the young can make great achievements'. CELAP employs a large number of young teachers for long-term development. As a result, many young teachers act as leaders of project groups, and many take on the role of '*banbu*' (class cadres in charge of other students), which is a crucial platform for young teachers to acquire adequate expertise. When it was first created, CELAP set up a team to demonstrate how to do pioneering work to rally teachers together. In recent years, the Teaching and Research Department has confirmed the training

theme and discussed the teaching focus of the internal department training for each spring and autumn term, which is beneficial in that it improves the quality and ability of teachers. CELAP also organizes teachers to study and take part in exchanges abroad. Since 2011, we have sent approximately 80 teachers to study in the USA in our collaboration with Procter & Gamble (P&G), which has effectively broadened the international horizons of our full-time teachers.

In order to meet the training requirements, CELAP insists on innovating the construction mechanism of teaching faculties in the aspects of responsibility, the incentive mechanism, the appraisal system and the logistics system to ensure successful development. First, we decide the responsibilities of our full-time teachers scientifically. Our full-time teachers are responsible for designing curricula, developing new courses, organizing classes and lecturing to ensure that training is conducted logically and smoothly. Second, we have set up a scientific development model to discover and cultivate talent. Following the principle of 'setting posts as required', having signed employment contracts and set their achievement goals, we give feedback punctually after tracking teachers' work regularly to promote their teaching performance. CELAP adopts an appraisal system for technical posts where socialized evaluation and employment are separated. We have set up a professional title appraisal and employment committee which consists of academy leaders, senior professors and people in charge from the sectors concerned, and is integrated with the working characteristics in the official education and training. We have also set the criteria for evaluation and employment. We make efforts to fully leverage the guiding role of the professional title appraisal system, to guide the teachers to commit to promoting teaching and scientific research, and to pave a professional development path for our teaching teams, especially for those who are young. This appraisal system has helped us promote more than 40 full-time teachers to senior technical posts. Third, we set up a logical evaluation system after experimenting and exploring. We are currently preparing to set up a mechanism for assessing the workload of teachers. In accordance with the principles of integrating process management with results-oriented management, annual assessment with employment-period assessment, and work achievement with developing potential, we have attempted to set up an evaluation system for teaching performance and a mechanism for assessing talent that fit the characteristics of official education and training, the subjects and the job requirements. For the successful development of teaching and scientific research, we refine work regulations, quantify the evaluation criteria, and scientifically assess teaching performance through teaching plans, the development of curricula and the employment of part-time teachers. Fourth, after experimentation CELAP has set up a sound remuneration welfare and service system. We attract, encourage and maintain excellent talent by setting up a salary system which is competitive and fair and by establishing a flexible welfare system. We offer regular interviews and consideration to teachers with difficulties while insisting on putting people first and integrating political work with compassion and care. We also offer active consultation for personnel and guidance for professional development to relieve the concerns of teachers about being separated from their spouses, and enabling their children to live and to join nurseries or schools in the cities where they work.

II. Part-time Teachers

1. A key component of official education and training faculties

Various excellent talented people from all walks of life are welcome to serve in the education and training of officials as part-time teachers. Their work complements that of full-time teachers, and ensures that the needs of different learners are met. This practice is an effective measure that improves teaching quality by taking full advantage of excellent social educational resources. In 2006, the *Regulations on Official Education and Training Work (Trial)* set the practice of integrating social resources as a fixed operation for recruiting official trainers. Specifically, it stipulates that training institutions should employ those with rich practical experience and high theoretical level to serve as part-time teachers, such as senior party and government leaders, entrepreneurs, well known scholars and experts at home or abroad, and that they should establish national and provincial (including autonomous regions and municipalities) reservoirs of teachers for talent sharing. In 2010, the *Reform Program* added competitive elements to the teacher recruitment system for both enrolment and dismissal of teachers. Local institutions lower than city-level should gradually come to take part-time teachers as their main training force. Senior officials especially should themselves participate in the work to give lectures or presentations to trainees. Higher-level institutions should send their outstanding teachers to lower-level institutions to conduct teaching or training work. By 2020, the Organization Department of the CPC Central Committee and provincial organization departments should have platforms set up for talent sharing through the construction of national and provincial reservoirs of teachers.

Until now, we have pooled a considerable amount of part-time teachers to meet the requirements of official training at all levels. In practice, senior party and government leaders, entrepreneurs, well known scholars and experts at home and abroad are invited to training institutions to give presentations, examine case studies, and share their experience. The *Regulations on Party Schools, Regulations on Schools of Administration, Regulations on Official Education and Training Work (Trial)* and other regulations all demand that local leaders play a role in their regional official training institutions, such as giving presentations or offering policy interpretations. Their frequent participation effectively supports local official training at all levels. For example, in the Central Party School, a member of the Standing Committee of the Political Bureau of the CPC Central Committee functions as the president of the school and gives a presentation annually; top party and government leaders offer lectures to ministers and provincial leaders at the beginning of every year. In every province and municipality, the senior leaders also go to their party schools or schools of administration to deliver speeches to train their local officials.

The part-time teaching team is the pillar of official education and training in China, and part-time teachers in some institutions make up the majority in their faculty. For example, at CELAP, 90% of courses are taught

Descendants of Jinggangshan Red Army soldiers sharing revolutionary stories as part of a 'revolutionary education tourism' programme (Wang Yongji, Xinhua News Agency)

by part-time teachers to meet the needs of diverse trainees and to cover different subjects. Meanwhile, the full-time faculty members carry out their major tasks of developing new courses and contacting relevant leaders and experts to teach in the academy. They usually invite senior leaders from the CPC, ministers from the central government, well known entrepreneurs, officials from different regions, or various outstanding practitioners from all walks of life to participate in CELAP's leadership training. These have included: Liu Mingkang, former chairman of the China Securities Regulatory Commission, who often gave lectures or guided young teachers to conduct research on finance as a guest professor of CELAP; and Wu Renbao, former party secretary of Huaxi Village in Jiangsu Province, who also came to give guest lectures, and who was very popular among his trainee audience. Furthermore, leaders from other countries, famous entrepreneurs, scholars and experts from the world's leading universities are invited to CELAP to work, and they have become a stable force to carry out CELAP's international leadership training programs. Part-time teachers therefore play a key role at CELAP.

As the *Reform Program* stipulates, local institutions lower than city-level should gradually take part-time teachers as their main staff for official training.

2. The construction of part-time teaching faculties

There are four main steps for the selection and recruitment of part-time teachers. The first step is to select competent teachers: choosing leaders, senior executives, experts at home or abroad with both rich experience and high theoretical level to serve in the education and training of officials according to relevant standards. The second is to recruit one as a faculty member: once they are employed, they will be granted the certificate as a guest lecturer. They will be introduced to the institution to familiarize themselves with their rights and duties as well as teaching requirements. The third is to fully utilize their talents: according to their expertise, teachers will be arranged to perform different teaching tasks and thus utilize their abilities systematically with clear teaching objectives. The last step is to assess and manage: every guest teacher will be assessed by their students and the host institution, and only those who excel may keep their post and continue to teach.

Case 9 CELAP Strongly Develops Teacher Resource Reservoir Construction

Drawing on experiences and setbacks from other prestigious training institutions at home and abroad, CELAP has been constructing its full-time teaching faculty with high standards and expanding its scope for selecting part-time teachers since its creation, in accordance with the principle of 'complementing full-time with part-time teachers, with the latter playing a major role' and the requirements of the CPC Central Committee. The academy's innovative management mechanism adopts the rule of usefulness to explore a new path for faculty development. The team is constituted with part-time teachers with a high theoretical level and rich practical experience, providing talent for fulfilling all of the tasks of the CPC Central Committee.

Our school recruits part-time teachers with a strict standard and a broad vision of our country in the world. In the recruitment of teachers, we choose leading party and government officials, managers of enterprises and prestigious professors and scholars as our part-time teachers to give lectures in our school. Our selection criteria demand a high theoretical level and rich practical experience. Step by step, we have set up a part-time teacher base that consists of more than 500 people, which is relatively stable and constantly optimized. We have also established an 'A and B supporting system' of part-time teachers for some important curricula (whereby teacher B can stand in for teacher A, if necessary). With the agreement that they do not need to be ours but can serve us, we equip some part-time teachers with assistant teachers to strengthen our connection with them. We effectively communicate ideas and prepare lessons together before class to set clear requirements, ensure good management and sufficient interaction in class by having students preside over class discussions to comment on lessons after they have been given; to give feedback, summary and improvement after class by giving out questionnaires and organizing seminars for students. Meanwhile, our school puts much emphasis on the idea that there is no forbidden area for research, yet there are disciplinary requirements in class, so part-time teachers must give lessons on the basis of alignment with our teaching objectives to ensure that they are teaching efficiently. On top of this, our school thoroughly administers those part-time teachers, therefore those who do not pass the evaluation standards of teaching quality are sifted out.

When recruiting part-time teachers, the steps taken are as follows: First, officials of intermediate and senior ranks are invited to give lessons at CELAP. In order to help the students grasp the policies of the party and country, our school invites senior leaders to give lectures according to the requirements of the courses. Many leaders who are at or above the ministerial and provincial level have given lectures at our school. Second, we endeavor to turn successful practitioners into teachers. We search for good teachers who are model practitioners in reform and opening up, and building modernization. Focusing on the teaching theme, the panel of the teaching project actively looks for typical representatives of all kinds in various ways, such as by following up news reports, recommendations from students and the sectors concerned, and social surveys. The panel then arranges for specially assigned staff to contact and investigate into their background and their experience, and sort the best from the group. Lastly, a teaching coordination meeting held in our academy or an office meeting of the president decides the part-time teachers who are to be recruited. Third, we choose part-time teachers from excellent students. These students come from all fields, and many of them are experts in a specialized field and have abundant leadership experience. We sort excellent students and test their teaching levels in a students' forum, invite them to give lessons after their graduation and eventually turn these excellent students into part-time teachers. In this way we follow the philosophy that those who are students today can be our faculty members tomorrow. Fourth, we recruit part-time teachers from leading figures in different fields. Based on training tasks and teaching requirements, we invite a group of leading figures in prestigious universities and research institutes in our country to act as part-time teachers or to give lessons in our academy by combining the teaching project panel's research and analysis together with the recommendation of insiders. Some leaders from other countries, famous scholars and senior entrepreneurs abroad are invited after the approval of the ministries concerned, such as the Ministry of Foreign Affairs, as we have to be active but prudent. More than 400 famous figures from abroad have given lectures in our school since the creation of the academy.

Teacher resource reservoirs of all levels, ranging in scale from national to local, have been established and highly valued for the mutual sharing of excellent teacher resources nationwide. A teacher resource reservoir is a center for gathering, storing, using and developing a database of teachers. Integrating various teaching resources can effectively and efficiently benefit official education and training all over the country. During this process, a couple of factors should be taken into consideration. They are: First, high quality. The management system of the training institutions should set standards for the input of excellent teaching resources to ensure the reservoir of resources is of high quality. Anyone who meets the standards can be enlisted in the reservoir of resources either by self-recommendation or organizational recommendation. Second, full utilization. We publicize information about teachers via networks to official training institutions at different levels for mutual sharing, so that they can invite teachers they need to implement their teaching curricula. Third, strict management: we check its application regularly, enrich and adjust the information punctually, and manage it flexibly.

Having excellent teachers is fundamental for improving the quality of official training. In 2010, the *Reform Program* set up the goal for the management reform of official teaching faculties, which included: adjusting recruitment, developing appraisal systems to meet the newly emerging demands of our national scientific development, to meet new expectations of leaders at various levels, and to meet the requirement of fully utilizing excellent talent. With such a target, these endeavors are made to promote management reform: First, optimizing teaching resources to retain the best talent; speeding up the socialization of the teaching faculty, increasing the proportion of part-time teachers, and in particular choosing among top party or government leaders, senior executives, well known experts and model workers to be guest lecturers; setting up national and provincial reservoirs of teacher resources for the exchange and sharing of excellent teaching resources. Second, reinforcing the training of teachers and improving their quality; carrying out projects on training official instructors, particularly the young and middle-aged teachers who function as the backbone of their school. They are usually sent to further their study, serve in temporary posts, do field research, or sit in classes so as to improve their practical ability to apply theory to practice. Third, evaluating objectively and managing unequivocally; making efforts to build professional ethics in official trainers and establishing a scientific appraisal system to introduce a competitive system to filter out anyone who is incompetent and maintain high-quality teachers. Furthermore, we make good use of assessment results for professional title assignments and post appointments in order to maintain the initiative and creativity of teachers.

The specific qualification requirements for official education and training of teachers are as follows.

First and foremost, they should possess good ideological quality and professional ethics. These teachers are supposed to keep closely in line with the principles of the CPC Central Committee theoretically and politically, and to uphold Marxism-Leninism, Mao Zedong Thought, Deng Xiaoping Theory, the important thoughts of the Three Represents, the Scientific Outlook on Development, and put into practice the guiding principles from Comrade Xi Jinping's major speeches. They should love their profession, devote themselves to the cause and work hard with strict discipline as good model scholars and educators.

Second, they should demonstrate a higher theoretical level. They must have a solid foundation of Marxist theory and be able to apply their Marxist stance and methods to specific problem analysis, and then guide their work in a spirit of developing Marxism. They should show a mastery of the party guidelines, principles and policies, and help build trainees' willingness and determination to engage in the party cause. They must also be good at connecting theory with practice, and instruct their students to solve realistic problems with acquired knowledge.

Third, they should have a good command of academic knowledge. Being knowledgeable is a necessity for teachers to teach in class and to conduct high-level research by gathering information on the latest developments in their own field and other relevant disciplines.

Fourth, they should have accumulated sufficient work experience, as their trainees are officials with substantial social and practical experience. It is a must for teachers to know a lot about the world, the country and the people, and to have a good command of information on our national reform and opening up, modernization, and the key development strategies and policies of the party and government.

Fifth, they should grasp modern methodology and techniques with knowledge of some basic laws, features and patterns of leadership training. They should be skillful at using various methods to cater to the diverse needs of different officials and thereby actively encourage participation in the training.

Last but not least, teachers are supposed to be competent in teaching and research. They should not only be good at teaching, but also be able to conduct research, with the ultimate goal of improving the teaching system by producing and applying more academic work.

Qualification Requirements for Official Education and Training Faculties

The *Regulations on Official Education and Training Work (Trial)* states that official education and training teachers should possess the following qualifications: good ideological quality and professional ethics, a high theoretical level, a solid command of academic knowledge, rich work experience, a grasp of modern pedagogical methodology and techniques, and competence in teaching and research.

The *Regulations on CPC Party Schools*: working staff in party schools should always keep in line with the CPC Central Committee, and possess the following qualities and capabilities: great communist ideals, firm belief in socialism with Chinese characteristics, loyalty to Marxism, a passion for party school education and observance of party discipline; a solid foundation in Marxist theory, a mastery over the CPC's line and policies, a good command of academic knowledge, an innovative spirit, and a capacity to explore crucial theories and tackle realistic problems. They should also be competent teachers with integrity and strict discipline, good role models, and should be good at conducting research, generalizing experiences, connecting theory with practice, and leadership training with modern methodology.

The *Regulations on Schools of Administration*: teachers in schools of administration must have the following capabilities and qualities: faith in socialism with Chinese characteristics, conformity with laws and regulations, high morality, integrity and professional ethics, a solid theoretical foundation, rich academic knowledge, a rigorous style of study, good capacity to teach, train and research, and consultative ability to decide on key policies.

Conclusion

All in all, the system of official education and training in China has been established with its own characteristics based on practical experience. Its main characteristics are as follows:

(1) Keeping in line with the principle of serving the party, working in the overall interests of the Chinese nation, and sustaining sound growth of officials

The education and training of Chinese officials is conducted under the leadership of the CPC, and aspires to develop highly qualified officials at all levels. Its vitality lies in its working principle of serving the cause of the party and the nation and acting in their overall interests. It is a primary, fundamental and strategic process to cultivate and continuously provide groups of good officials and talented people for the party and the country at every crucial development stage. To work toward the main targets of the party and the nation is a key lesson acquired by the party to implement official education and training. The training of officials has constantly adapted to changing needs, new historical orientations and new development requirements, playing an active and constructive role in promoting the cause of the party and the country. The education and training of officials is fundamental and strategic to the smooth development of the party and the nation, and it is the key to establishing a large contingent of high-caliber officials to continue the great construction of socialism with Chinese characteristics and new projects of the party.

Great importance has been attached to education and training for the sustainable and healthy development of Chinese officials. To take all party cadres and government officials as training subjects is a distinct feature of this process. Therefore, it covers three general types of officials, which are party and government cadres, business executives and senior professionals or technicians for an extensive and comprehensive education, with a focus on the backup forces and officials senior to the county and prefectural ranks. The extent and strength of the education and training of Chinese officials is distinguished globally in terms of its methods for leadership development.

The selection and training processes are equally important in establishing a large group of quality officials. As stated above, training is a crucial procedure and is often a prerequisite for promotion to a leading position. Even if an official has not attained the qualifications required by the education and training, he or she must take remedial courses after the promotion.

(2) Combine theoretical orthodoxy with education in party spirit and raising competence

Marxism is an essential guide for the governance of the party and the nation, a powerful psychological weapon to transform both the material and spiritual world, and the spiritual core of CPC members. The CPC has been incorporating Marxism with Chinese characteristics throughout the long struggles for revolution, construction and reform of the country, and has produced successive related theories such as Mao Zedong Thought, Deng Xiaoping Theory, the important thoughts of the Three Represents, the Scientific Outlook on Development and the guiding principles from Comrade Xi Jinping's major speeches. Theoretical education has long been a keen practice of official training which updates the knowledge of leaders with the appropriation of Marxism in China, and thus training institutions promptly disseminate every new addition to political theory. In official education and training, the latest development of Marxism in the Chinese context has been taken as the core component of the teaching curriculum, and has been embedded in new course books, introduced into classes, and ingrained into the minds of officials to help them adopt Marxist values and a Marxist view of the world. By doing so, officials may keep their advanced standpoint as CPC members with political enthusiasm and determination, which is a significant effect of official education and training. The development of governing capacity is vital to the party and an important objective of official training and practice, so the elevation of the competence of officials to lead is a main task which is carried through in all training activities. It is proven that the party's governing capacity can be continuously enhanced as long as it is promoted consistently through the processes of official education and training with diverse and dynamic experiences and activities.

(3) Continuing to practice coordinated management with macro-supervision

The CPC has always emphasized the coordinated management of official education and training. Initially, it was under the management of the Official Education Department founded by the Central Committee, but was later transferred to the Central Publicity and Education Department. Currently, official education and training is under the direct administration of the Central Organization Department, with different tasks allocated to different divisions, implemented by training institutions in different localities all over the country. To enforce macro-supervision and coordinated management, a system of joint conferences has been set up by the Central Organization Department to negotiate the work of different training institutions among their administrators. The central coordination facilitates training practices at different levels with the support of various powers and resources, and effectively pushes ahead the scientific development of Chinese official education and training.

(4) Striving incessantly to perfect the system and consolidate the foundation

Great attention has also been paid to the system development of official education and training so as to carry through its tasks scientifically, based on regulations and standards. For example, systems of on-the-job education and full-time training were operated early on in the Yan'an Period. After the founding of the PRC, refresher training and theoretical study were set up to raise cadres' theoretical quality and enrich their knowledge. Since the beginning of the process of reform and opening up, and especially after the 16th National Congress of the CPC, we have been making concerted efforts to reinforce the structure of the system and have established a comparatively comprehensive system. In January 2006, the CPC Central Committee issued the *Regulations on Official Education and Training Work (Trial)*, which was the first CPC official regulation on national official education and training. Later, the CPC Central Committee and the State Council launched a series of regulations in support of the work, namely: the *Regulations on CPC Party Schools;* the *Regulations on Schools of Administration*; the *Regulations on Civil Servant Training*; and the *Reform Program for Official Education and Training from 2010 to 2020*. In addition, a Five-year Plan is formulated every five years to accommodate the demands for the development of official education and training for the cause of the party and the nation. Practice has shown that strengthening the structure of the system is an effective measure to guide the education and training of officials over a long period, so we should continue our work to make the training more scientific, systematic and standardized.

In addition, efforts are made to establish training bases, recruit teachers, develop textbooks and pool funds for the sustainable development and continuous growth of Chinese official education and training. Working unremittingly to consolidate the fundamental features and perfect the overall system is a feature of Chinese leadership training programs that distinguishes them from those of other countries, and results in a solid foundation for the development of quality officials through complementary channels and diverse institutions. A new plan for the state-level official education and training system came into being in 2005 with the opening of three academies: CELAP, CELAJ and CELAY, in addition to two former academies, the Party School of the CPC Central Committee (The Central Party School) and Chinese Academy of Governance. A national hierarchical training network with training institutions at different levels and also for different professionals was also established to meet diversified demands. We then developed different types of training organs such as party schools in government departments and enterprises, schools of administration, cadre schools, workers' schools, training centers, official training programs held by higher learning institutions, social leadership training programs and schools. These operations complement each other, partly resolve the funding problem, promote competition, and enhance training efficiency.

The Central Organization Department organizes experts to work on the development of books and then arranges to have four series of books published. Top leaders from the central government also pay keen attention to books and contribute to them. For instance, in August 2006, Hu Jintao, General Secretary of the CPC at the time wrote the preface of the second national series of books for official education and training; then in August 2011, he wrote another preface for a textbook of case studies on scientific development. In the latter he emphasized that we should uphold Deng Xiaoping Theory, the important thoughts of Three Represents and the Scientific Outlook on Development to equip the minds of officials, speed up the growth of the CPC as a political party based on the study of Marxism, and cultivate a contingent of high-caliber officials to promote the scientific and harmonious development of Chinese society. In October 2015, General Secretary Xi Jinping composed the foreword to the fourth national series of textbooks for official education and training, in which he stressed that leading officials should deepen their understanding of the guiding principles of the 18th National Congress of the CPC and the third and fourth plenary sessions of the 18th CPC Central Committee. He said that they should also further their studies on and carry out the working plans and requirements of the CPC Central Committee, and strengthen their confidence in the path, theory and system of socialism with Chinese characteristics. He emphasized that leading officials should endeavour to become more knowledgeable, more professionally competent, more responsible and more capable while performing their duties.

Official education and training at different levels is funded hierarchically by its corresponding government, and its budget grows with the rise of local government revenue.

(5) Keep pace with the times, reform and innovation

Reform and innovation are important for maintaining the vitality of official education and training in China. History shows that emancipation of the mind to keep pace with the times and to reform and innovate lies at the core of this undertaking, and is the key driver of development from nothing to the current scale, and from immaturity to maturity Since the founding of the PRC, more standardized and systematized methods have been adopted to cater to the demands of national economic and social development. In particular, since the beginning of reform and opening up, we have started to draw on the effective measures and successful experiences from the leadership training practices of developed countries, and have thereby resolved our own problems over time. A new system of official education and training has come into being since then, with a new training ideology, new content, new methods and new management in a spirit of being enterprising and innovative. As Hu Jintao once stated, we must "renew training content, improve training methodology, integrate training resources, and optimize training staff", and "chart a new path of innovation in a realistic context, to secure solid effects by reinforced training". Accordingly, reform and innovation are highlighted in the *Reform Program for Official Education and Training from 2010 to 2020* with a blueprint for the process over those 10 years, which demonstrates clear benefits in that the continuous growth of education and training accommodates the development of the party and the nation. Practice proves that a basic method to achieve substantial results is to develop training theory, enrich practical experience, and perfect the training system to push reform and innovation forward by investigating new situations and solving new problems. By constantly reinvigorating its theory, content, methods and management mechanism, we will continuously improve Chinese official education and training with 'reform and innovation' as its central driving force.

Chapter Follow-up Questions and References

Introduction

Questions:

1. As to official education and training in China, what aspects do you want to know about the most?
2. What do you think is the relationship between official education and training and the fast development of China?

References:

1. Li Xiaosan, *A Brief History of CPC Cadre Education*, Beijing: Central CPC History Press, January 2009
2. Feng Jun, *Reform and Innovation in Official Education and Training*, Beijing: People's Publishing House, January 2011

Chapter 1

Questions:

1. What do you think are the characteristics of the management system of official education and training in China?
2. What is inspiring or worthwhile in the management system of official education and training in China?

References:

1. Official Education Bureau of the Organization Department of the CPC Central Committee, *Study Guidance for Regulations on Official Education and Training Work (Trial)*, Beijing: Party Building Book Publishing House, March 2006
2. Official Education Bureau of the Organization Department of the

CPC Central Committee, *A Collection of Special Reports on Reform and Innovation of the Official Education and Training System*, Beijing: Party Building Book Publishing House, December 2008
3. Feng Jun, *Reform and Innovation in Official Education and Training*, Beijing: People's Publishing House, January 2011
4. Official Education Bureau of the Organization Department of the CPC Central Committee, *Reading on Official Education Work*, Beijing: Party Building Book Publishing House, 2012
5. Official Education Bureau of the Organization Department of the CPC Central Committee, *21 Special Reports on Official Education and Training* (Vol. 1&2), Beijing: Party Building Book Publishing House, August 2013

Chapter 2

Questions:

1. How do you think China has made the methods of official education and training relevant to its content?
2. Compared with the training of officials in other countries, what do you find worth learning from the methods of official education and training in China?

References:

1. Official Education Bureau of the Organization Department of the CPC Central Committee, *Study Guidance to Regulations on Official Education and Training Work (Trial)*, Beijing: Party Building Books Publishing House, March 2006
2. Official Education Bureau of the Organization Department of the CPC Central Committee, *A Collection of Special Reports on the Reform and Innovation of the Official Education and Training System*, Beijing: Party Building Books Publishing House, December 2008
3. Feng Jun, *Reform and Innovation in Official Education and Training*, Beijing: People's Publishing House, January 2011
4. Official Education Bureau of the Organization Department of the CPC Central Committee, *Readings on Official Education Work*, Beijing: Party Building Books Publishing House, 2012
5. Official Education Bureau of the Organization Department of the

CPC Central Committee, *21 Special Reports on Official Education and Training* (Vol. 1&2), Beijing: Party Building Books Publishing House, August 2013

Chapter 3

Questions:

1. How do you think China has made the methods of official education and training relevant to its content?
2. Compared with training in other countries, what have you found worth learning from the methods of official education and training in China?

References:

1. Official Education Bureau of the Organization Department of the CPC Central Committee, *Study Guidance to Regulations on Official Education and Training Work (Trial)*, Beijing: Party Building Books Publishing House, March 2006
2. Official Education Bureau of the Organization Department of the CPC Central Committee, *A Collection of Special Reports on Reform and Innovation of the Official Education and Training System*, Beijing: Party Building Books Publishing House, December 2008
3. Feng Jun, *Reform and Innovation in Official Education and Training*, Beijing: People's Publishing House, January 2011
4. Official Education Bureau of the Organization Department of the CPC Central Committee, *Readings on Official Education Work*, Beijing: Party Building Books Publishing House, 2012
5. Official Education Bureau of the Organization Department of the CPC Central Committee, *21 Special Reports on Official Education and Training* (Vol. 1&2), Beijing: Party Building Books Publishing House, August 2013

Chapter 4

Questions:

1. What do you think are the characteristics of the structure of official education and training institutions in China?
2. What measures do you think China has taken to improve and revitalize its operation of official education and training institutions?

References:

1. Circular of the General Office of the CPC Central Committee for Issuing *2010-2020 Reform Program for Official Education and Training*, (No. 18 [2010])
2. Circular of the CPC Central Committee for Issuing *Regulations on CPC Party Schools*, (No. 13 [2008] September 3, 2008)
3. *Regulations on the Work of Schools of Administration*, (passed at the 92nd executive meeting of the State Council on December 14, 2009)

Chapter 5

Questions:

1. What are the features of the development of the teaching faculties of official education and training in China?
2. What do you think of the measures for the development of the teaching faculties of official education and training in China? How would you practice them at work?

References:

1. Official Education Bureau of the Organization Department of the CPC Central Committee, *Study Guidance to Regulations on Official Education and Training Work (Trial)*, Beijing: Party Building Books Publishing House, March 2006
2. Official Education Bureau of the Organization Department of the CPC Central Committee, *Readings on Official Education Work*, Beijing: Party Building Books Publishing House, 2012
3. Circular of the General Office of the CPC Central Committee for Issuing *2010-2020 Reform Program for Official Education and Training*, (No. 18 [2010])
4. Circular of the CPC Central Committee for Issuing *Regulations on CPC Party Schools*, (No. 13 [2008], September 3, 2008)
5. *Regulations on the Work of Schools of Administration*, (passed at the 92nd executive meeting of the State Council on December 14, 2009)

Conclusion

Questions:

1. Which Chinese practices and experiences do you think are worth learning from and following in the education and training of officials?

2. What are the major features of official education and training in China?

References:

1. Official Education Bureau of the Organization Department of the CPC Central Committee, *Study Guidance to Regulations on Official Education and Training Work (Trial)*, Beijing: Party Building Books Publishing House, March 2006
2. Gao Shiqi, Zhang Jiasheng, *Review and Reflection on the Education and Training of Party Cadres over the Past 90 Years, Zhongguo Zuzhi Renshi Bao (China Human Resources Organization Newspaper)*, July 8, 2011
3. Feng Jun, *Five Relations Should be Handled Well in Official Education and Training, Study Times*, December 20, 2010
4. Feng Jun, *Experiential Knowledge on Official Education and Training, Guangming Daily*, August 20, 2012
5. Feng Jun, *The Historical Evolution and Primary Experience of Official Education and Training Since the Founding of the PRC, A Research Anthology of Studies on the Past 60 Years after the Founding of the PRC*, Beijing: Central Party Literature Press, October 2009